# SETTLEMENT AND UNSETTLEMENT
# IN EARLY AMERICA

*The crisis of political legitimacy*
*before the Revolution*

# Settlement and unsettlement in early America

## The crisis of political legitimacy before the Revolution

KENNETH A. LOCKRIDGE

*Department of History*
*University of Michigan*

CAMBRIDGE UNIVERSITY PRESS

CAMBRIDGE

LONDON   NEW YORK   NEW ROCHELLE
SYDNEY   MELBOURNE

Published by the Press Syndicate of the University of Cambridge
The Pitt Building, Trumpington Street, Cambridge CB2 IRP
32 East 57th Street, New York, NY 10022, USA
296 Beaconsfield Parade, Middle Park, Melbourne 3206, Australia

First published 1981

Printed in the United States of America
Typeset and printed by Heritage Printers, Inc., Charlotte, North Carolina
Bound by the Delmar Company, Charlotte, North Carolina

*Library of Congress Cataloging in Publication Data*
Lockridge, Kenneth A
Settlement and unsettlement in early America.
(The Joanne Goodman lecture series)
Bibliography: p.
1. United States – Politics and government – Colonial
period, ca. 1600–1775 – Addresses, essays, lectures.
I. Title. II. Series: Joanne Goodman lecture series.
E188.5.L62   973.2   80–25658
ISBN 0 521 23707 6

The Joanne Goodman Lecture Series
has been established by Joanne's family and friends
to perpetuate the memory of her blithe spirit,
her quest for knowledge, and the rewarding years
she spent at the University of Western Ontario

# *Contents*

# Preface

EVERY historian welcomes a chance to put together the history of his period in a way which
makes sense to him. An invitation to give a set of lectures usually provides the occasion, and in this case
special gratitude goes to Edwin A. Goodman and to
Neville Thompson for the opportunity to develop
these ideas in the 1980 Goodman Lectures at the University of Western Ontario. The dedication to this
book explains the purpose of this lecture series and
suggests the warmth which characterizes the occasion. Rhys Isaac, Neville Thompson, Ian Steele, and
Harold and Jackie Livesay have improved this essay
throughout its gestation. If it, like all reachings for
large generalization, remains incomplete, that is no
fault of these friends or of the readers for Cambridge
University Press. Their efforts have helped create the
scaffolding of an interpretation which might be filled
in in detail in a larger work. Finally, sincere thanks
are due to Debbie Lanyi and Mary Poerner for editorial help.

Ann Arbor, Michigan
January, 1981      KENNETH A. LOCKRIDGE

# Introduction

IN 1607 several dozen Englishmen settled at James-town in Virginia. By 1776 two and one-half mil-lion Americans were involved in a revolution against British rule, a revolution which proved to be more revolutionary than many had intended. From this point on, the main lines of American history are clear. Washington was succeeded by Jefferson and Jefferson by Jackson as, president by president, both before and after the Civil War, Americans marched willingly or reluctantly into the modern age. One hundred and seventy years of colonial history largely without structure or theme are soon forgotten in the welter of events that followed upon the Declaration of Independence, the Constitution, and the presiden-cy of George Washington. Yet those long colonial years made the Revolution and all that followed pos-sible and stamped the new nation irretrievably.

It is the job of the colonial historian to give coher-ence to incoherence in order that Americans may understand themselves better. Rising to this chal-lenge, previous generations of historians have sug-gested the main themes of the colonial era. They have pointed out that Americans were independent,

religious, democratic, enterprising, and individualistic from the beginning, long before the Revolution.
There is no reason to quarrel with these conclusions,
or with still other analyses which have traced to the
colonial era enduring conflicts over the distribution
of power and of economic resources between elites
and non-elites, native-born Americans and immi-
grants, Yankees and Southerners. In all these ways
the colonial past contained the germ of the American
future. The colonial era is, in these senses, no mystery
at all.

Yet the way people three hundred years ago perceived their world is bound to remain in some degree
a mystery. So many persons, so long dead, so many
of whom left no record of their thoughts, must remain
an eternally fascinating puzzle. Many new volumes
of printed documents from the colonial era offer
better access than ever before to the mental world of
colonial Americans. Simultaneously, the kinds of
sources historians are willing to consider and the ways
they use these sources have expanded greatly in recent years. What was once called "intellectual history" has broadened into an enquiry into the way
people saw their environment and responded to its
challenges. For these reasons there is more cause than
ever before to look anew into the attitudes of colonial
Americans. This essay is one attempt to penetrate
their mental world, using the sources and sensitivities
of the latest generation of American historical schol-

arship. It is an effort to reach for the themes inherent in this world. It is not original because it owes so great a debt to such current historians as John Demos, Timothy Breen, Paul Boyer and Stephen Nissenbaum, Edmund S. Morgan, Rhys Isaac, and Gordon Wood. Rather, it is a personal synthesis written out of the delight which many historians have created in the history of early America.

What emerges on looking closely into the statements of the colonists themselves is that the colonial era was marked by a fruitless struggle to achieve a legitimate political order. In New England, the Puritans began by defining themselves to the brink of perfection. Every leader, every town, every ordinary individual was to seek that precise balance of social qualities which would assure both order and divine approval. But already by the end of the seventeenth century this delicately poised order had lapsed into two quite different views of the world, one hierarchical and the other localistic. Each of these views or principles strove for acceptance, and so for legitimacy, in a struggle which ran through the subsequent history of colonial New England. Their struggle emerged in explicit form in the course of the American Revolution. In Virginia and elsewhere in the South, the English settlements first manifested a chaotic individualism which was destructive of all public order. Here for a long time the problem was to evolve any principle of political order with a shred of a claim to legitimacy. By the middle of the eighteenth century, native gentlemen had emerged atop a hierarchy of social and political authorities and had been widely accepted by the populace. But these gentlemen were in turn immediately challenged by an evangelical localism rather similar to that in New England, which rejected all their pretensions and which strove in turn to establish its own legitimacy. Here also the struggle continued into the Revolution.

The convergence of New England and of Virginia and the colonial South is one of the more remarkable features of the colonial world. By the time of the American Revolution each area could be characterized in terms of a similar struggle between two principles – one pious and localistic, the other worldly and hierarchical – both striving for legitimacy and neither able to succeed in the face of a skeptical environment and the claims of its rival. By the time of the Revolution, Americans elsewhere had also embraced one or another version of these two contending principles. They also were to suffer from the failure of either principle to achieve full legitimacy. All over America the Revolution saw a more dramatic playing out of this rivalry of localism and hierarchy and of this dilemma of failed legitimacies. Early Americans' inability to agree on a single principle of social and political order was to become hauntingly familiar to later generations of Americans. In the midst of revolution, however, some Americans were already reaching for a more sophisticated conception of their social and political order better suited to a new age.

# Puritan New England

BUILDING a legitimate social and political order in Massachusetts should have been easy for
the Puritans. They knew exactly what they did not
want. They did not want the individualistic, competitive, commercialized, ruthlessly hierarchical social
world or the centralizing state characteristic of the
Renaissance England whence they fled. By implication, they wanted a social world based on communal
love in which a modest degree of social hierarchy and
of state power would ensure political order. This
blend of human decency with social order was what
God asked of men, and New England offered no ob-
stacle to their plans.

Surely and swiftly they constructed a social order
which blended community and hierarchy in the name
of divine perfection, and they expressed their longing
for God's perfection still more energetically in a
church made up only of accepted saints. Where was
the problem, then? The problem was that the Puritan
experiment decayed as surely as all human construc-
tions. This is a known story. Slowly the corruptions
of England revisited the little society so carefully
wrought, until it became a mere province of England.

What the story seldom encompasses, however, is the resistance of a segment of the New England population to accommodations with commercial development, with overarching social hierarchies, or with the overweening power of the state. A localism conceived in England and tempered in the fires of witchcraft held out for many decades against the inevitable future.

For the New England landscape had given refuge to many villagers eager to realize the Puritan dream of human decency in a local context and with only a bare modicum of social hierarchy. Snug in their new villages, they saw no reason to abandon paradise for the pretensions of an anglicizing world. Those who would accommodate themselves to a striving, commercial, competitive society directed by a vastly elevated elite from a metropolis – be it London, or Boston, or, later, Washington – faced the stubborn resistance of these villagers, who by now equated community with God and self-sufficiency with virtue. Submerged until the time of the American Revolution, the silent struggle between those stubborn localists and the more worldly hierarchs burst into the open in the midst of the War for Independence. It suddenly became clear that for many years New England had had not one but two social and political visions, and that neither had achieved entire legitimacy.

RENAISSANCE EUROPE was an overwhelming experience for many of the men and women who survived it. It sent the Puritans scurrying first to the Bible and then, in some cases, to America. For the Renaissance was more than a rebirth of classical culture, or the discovery of perspective in painting, or the awakening of a new sense of human self-confidence. Spreading northward from Italy in the sixteenth and seventeenth centuries, the Renaissance was also a self-confidence bordering on arrogance. It was the preening arrogance of the swashbuckling goldsmith Benvenuto Cellini, whose autobiography screamed "me, me, me" at the expense of uncounted victims. It was the cynical arrogance of Machiavelli's idealized *Prince*, as echoed in the vicious statecraft of Francois I, of Gustav Vasa, and of Henry VIII. The Renaissance was also a western Europe revivified after the decimations of the Great Plague, its population waxing to levels unknown for two centuries, its cities fat with trade, its peasants free to strive for land, and its lords equally free to turn out their former serfs and replace them with sheep. The Renaissance was a Europe beginning to feel itself overcrowded and to see everywhere frantic struggles for a place in life.

Certainly that was the opinion of Sir Thomas More, the gifted Catholic reformer. While Luther was defending his theses in Germany, More was decrying the ruthlessness of his times in England, and agonizing over a church which did so little to alleviate the resultant suffering. In the preface to his *Utopia* More described one aspect of this ruthlessness, an English society mad for profits from wool: "Forsooth, quoth I, your sheep, which were wont to be so meek and tame, now eat up and swallow down the very men themselves. They consume and destroy whole fields, houses, and cities. For look, in what part of the realm doth grow the finest and therefore dearest wool, there noblemen and gentlemen, yea, even certain abbots, holy men God wot, not contenting themselves with the profits that were wont to go to their forefathers and predecessors, leave no ground for tillage; they enclose all into pastures, leaving nothing standing but only the church, to make of it a sheephouse. Therefore husbandmen be thrust out, either by fraud or by oppression or by wrongs and injuries. They must needs depart away, poor wretched silly souls, men, women, husbands, wives, fatherless children, widows, woeful mothers with their young babes, their whole households small in substance and much in number; away they trudge, finding no place to rest in. For one shepherd or herdsman is enough to eat up that ground with sheep or cattle, the occupying whereof with husbandry many were requisite.

Yea, besides this the price of wool is so risen that poor folk, which were wont to work it and make cloth of it, be now able to buy none at all. And this means very many be fair to forsake work and to give themselves to idleness. For the sheep being almost all come into rich men's hands, whom no need forceth to sell before they will, these will not sell before they may sell as dear as they want.

Now, to this wretched beggary and miserable poverty is joined great wantonness, importunate superfluity, and excessive riot. For not only gentleman's servants, but also handicraft men, yea, and almost the ploughmen of the country, [show] much strange and proud newfangleness in their apparel, and too much prodigal riot and sumptuous fare at their table. Cast out these pernicious abominations; make a law that they which plucked down farms and towns of husbandry shall build them up again. Let not so many be brought up in idleness, let husbandry and tillage be restored again, let cloth-working be renewed, that they may be honest labors."*

* Editorial note: In rendering the quotations for this book, I have followed the policy of the *William and Mary Quarterly* in not indenting or single-spacing such excerpts and have accepted the convention of Samuel Eliot Morison, in his edition of William Bradford's *Of Plymouth Plantation* (New York, 1952, 1967), in adopting modern usage regarding capitalization, punctuation, and spelling. As in the original models for these policies, the aim is a more readable text. Beyond this, the sentences quoted are intact, save where significant exceptions have been noted by an ellipsis. Any

More had had enough of the human costs of his swelling age in England. His book was a virtual plea for a place in which men could again live in a decent harmony with the land and with one another. Having little hope that the Catholic church he knew would create such a haven on earth, he established one in his imagination, on an island off the coast of South America. He called it Utopia.

A century later even Captain John Smith, that boldest of Renaissance rogues, could see the consequences of an England in which too many people were too brutally striving. On his return from New England in 1616, he asked his countrymen: "Who would live at home by consuming that which his friends go worthily? Or [merely] to maintain a silly show of bravery toil out thy heart, soul, and time basely, by shifts, tricks, cards, and dice? Or by relating news of others actions, shark here and there for a dinner; [or] deceive thy friends by fair promises and dissimulation, in borrowing where thou never intendest to pay? [Who would] offend the laws, burden

words added for clarification are in brackets. In one case capitalization and in another original spelling have been retained for emphasis.

Modern editions of *Utopia* vary greatly. The quotation used here represents a synthesis of these. To get an idea of the variation among editions, look at the Norton Critical Edition (New York, 1975). The best standard work is the *Yale Edition of the Complete Works of St. Thomas More*, Volume 4, edited by Edward Surtz, S. J., and J. H. Hexter, 1965.

thy Country, abuse thy self, despair in want, couzen thy kindred, yea, even thy own brother, and wish thy parents death (I will not say damnation) to have their estates?"

By Smith's day even this unscrupulous rogue had seen enough. Whether because of enclosing sheep owners or from the overwhelming growth of the population, still too many men could not make a living. They wished secretly that their parents would die, so that they could get land. They envisaged their parents' damnation and so earned their own. Others tried to live off those who had money by sharking dinners in exchange for cleverness, or by lying, or gaming, or cheating. The Renaissance had its own Dance of Death. Why not, Smith said, live instead in his New England?

Neither More nor Smith turned Puritan, but in this light it is possible to see why Puritanism grew in England and perhaps why all forms of Protestantism advanced throughout Renaissance Europe. In the face of a crowded, competitive, and not a little bit guilty society the reformed preachers offered an absolute God, whose Word told men to live in love, charity, and decency, and who guided them to salvation from sin, striving, and guilt. Protestantism became an inner migration for those who could not go to a New World.

Much of the nature of the Protestant, or certainly of the Puritan response, becomes clearer when seen in this light. In England, Puritanism was a world in which the "arminian" strivings of mankind were left behind. Not only the invented hierarchies of archbishops, bishops, and deans, reinforced by pompous ceremonies not found in the Bible, but also all that smacked of man's will was abandoned. Listeners strove to hear the famous preachers describe instead God's will, and sought to live as he prescribed, suppressing as sinful the smallest vestige of their own wills. Their inner migration ultimately involved a surrender of the self to God. "Broken-hearted" Christians eagerly received the message that he only wanted them to have faith and to live with their fellowmen in love. As they sought one another's company and aided each other in seeking these ends, often there grew a conviction that they might be in harmony with the Lord. Out of this came a sense of grace which was the freedom they had sought.

Puritans also sought, however, to extend God's order to all of England. Their divines had created a body of ideology on the nature of God, of the church, and of society which became the cutting edge for a Puritan conviction that England must absorb the Bible order or all would die. "We are the chariot and horsemen of Israel, that stand in the gap," lowered the Reverend Charles Chauncy. They did more than stand, they attacked. Chauncy once refused to take communion to a dying Anglican on the grounds that the Bible did not justify it, thus purifying the poor man in spite of himself. Clear on the nature of God, firm on how men were to live, though not always certain of all details of their ideal, Puritans soon advanced on the English church and on Parliament. When in the 1620s it appeared that the Puritan assault would fail, so great was their fear of spiritual and social disorder that they gave themselves over to despair, sure that God's wrath would descend upon all. It was this Puritanism which turned at last to a literal New World, in the form of New England.

Some Puritan pamphleteers for New England, such as Robert Cushman, simply took up the cry sounded first by More and then by Smith. The description of English society was familiar and so was the solution: namely, to go into that good and empty New England and live as God intended: "The straitness of the place is such as each man is fain to pluck his means as it were out of his neighbor's throat. There is such pressing and oppressing in towns and country about farms, trade, traffic, etc., so as a man can hardly set up anywhere but he shall pull down two of his neighbors. Many there are who get their living bearing burdens, multitudes get their means of life by prating, and so do numbers more by begging. Neither come these straits upon men always through intemperance, ill husbandry, indiscretion, etc., as some think, but even the most wise, sober, and discreet men go often to the wall when they have done their best. It is easy to see that the straitness of the place . . . cannot but produce such effects more and more. And they also, which now live sweetly, hardly will see their children attain to that privilege, but some circumventor or other will outstrip them and make them sit in the dust. Every . . . man should be ready to say with father Abraham, "Take thou the right hand and I will take the left"; let us not thus oppress, straighten, and afflict one another, but seeing there is a spacious land, the way to which is through the sea, we will end this difference in a day."

Yet more militant Puritan preachers, among them Charles Chauncy, had more in mind than More's pagan commonwealth or Smith's brave and open land, or Cushman's refuge from straitness and indecency. Chauncy said in effect that if the Church of England continued to resist the right practice of God's way, his people would go to New England to build in all its as yet unspecified details their Holy Order. This is what some meant when they spoke of New England as their garden.

❧

So they came to New England. Some, like Cushman, were men whose piety was nearly Anglican but who were determined to restore to their lives the decency, quiet, and order which had been robbed from them in England. In their eyes, God had ordained this for man. Others, like Chauncy, took a return to the Word of God more seriously; these would seek social and religious perfection with a ferocity and a desire for control which revealed deep resentments. Both would call New England their garden. As such different men worked together the garden would acquire a sensible balance of communal love and hierarchical order, beneath which lay a deep and ultimately vulnerable perfectionism.

John Winthrop had described the colony as a "City Upon a Hill" in his lecture "A Model of Christian Charity," delivered aboard the *Arabella* on the way to New England. It was Winthrop who, in this lecture, first disclosed that mixture of community and hierarchy which would characterize the new order. "God Almighty," began Winthrop, "hath so disposed of the condition of mankind, as in all times some must be rich and some poor, some high and eminent in power and dignity, others mean and in subjection." The good governor then explained the reasons for this, above all that "the preservation and good of the whole" was best served by these differences. For in this way God might "have the more occasion to manifest the work of his Spirit . . . in restraining: so that the rich and the mighty should not eat up the poor, nor the poor and despised rise up against their superiors and shake off their yoke." Further, not only God's restraining hand but also his very grace itself worked upon the social hierarchy to turn it from potential conflict to actual order: "as in the great ones [who respond with] love, mercy, gentleness, temperance, etc., [and] the poor and inferior sort

[with] faith, patience, obedience, etc." Furthermore, in the great hierarchy of social duties "every man [hath] need of other[s], and from hence they might all be knit more nearly together in the bond of brotherly affection."

The burden of the rest of the lecture was that justice and mercy had, nonetheless, to prevail between all members of society. As "a company professing ourselves fellow members of Christ," the settlers ought especially to be "knit together by that bond of [Christian] love," charity, and mercy which God's grace permitted. Without this commonality, all would be lost: "For the work we have in hand, is by a mutual consent through a special overruling providence, . . . to seek out a place of cohabitation and consortship under a due form of government both civil and ecclesiastical. In such cases the care of the public must oversway all private respects. The end is to improve our lives to do more service to the Lord, . . . that [we] ourselves and our posterity may . . . work out our salvation under the power and purity of his holy ordinances. [As] for the means whereby this may be effected, . . . we must not content ourselves with usual ordinary means. That which most in their Churches maintain as a truth in profession only, we must bring into familiar and constant practice, as in this duty of brotherly love. We must love one another with a pure heart, fervently; we must bear one another's burdens. The only way to avoid shipwreck . . . is to do justly, to love mercy, to walk humbly with our God; for this end we must be knit together as one man, we must be willing to abridge our selves of our superfluities, . . . make others conditions our own, rejoice together, mourn together, labor and suffer together. Always having before our eyes . . . our Community as members of the same body, so we shall keep the unity of the spirit in the bond of peace."

To a perceptible degree these instructions were carried out in practice. Most towns founded during Winthrop's lifetime wrote covenants and bylaws committing the members of each community to a miniature version of his balance between commonality and hierarchy. The founders of Springfield, Massachusetts, for example, promised first "to procure some Godly and faithful minister with whom we purpose to join in church covenant to walk in all the ways of Christ." Within this spiritual union there would be both "rich and poor." The original settlers were granted as much as ten times the amount of land given later and more ordinary men. This was because the former had "constantly continued to prosecute this plantation when others fell off for fear of the difficulties"; nonetheless, the result was the re-creation of a social hierarchy here in the wilderness. Likewise men of estate, who tended to invest heavily in cattle, were given extra shares of meadowland. They were "most apt to use such ground," but through this recognition their wealth and standing were buttressed. The same sorts of men were chosen leaders of the town. Yet beyond this every policy was bent toward commonality. Except for these few, differences in landholdings were small, and were chiefly related to the size of the family a man and his sons had to feed. "Everyone" received nearly equal strips in huge fields of arable, meadow, and woodland where men would labor close beside their neighbors. The tax structure was made as equitable as possible, and included rebates for those whose land was farthest from the center of the town so that they might not feel exploited by the community. Compared to the vast distances of the English social hierarchy, Springfield was an experiment in controlled similarity.

Springfield's social universe was fixed, as well: "Our town shall be composed of forty families or, if we think meet to alter our purpose, . . . not to exceed the number of fifty families." It was unalterable except unanimously: "[These] articles and orders [are] to be observed and kept by us and by our successors except we and every [one] of us for ourselves and in our own persons shall think meet upon better reason to alter our present resolutions." It was for forever, binding "us and our successors." Controlled by a degree of hierarchy and wrapped in the deep commonalities of their community, walking together in

Christ and literally together on the land, the men of Springfield had made an eternal order, a garden.

A similar balancing of community and hierarchy occurred in Winthrop's political theory, and here again there is evidence that the settlers shared his views. In Winthrop's view, the community of all men in their Christian enterprise needed to be expressed and strengthened through the election of leaders. So all men – or, once the ministers arrived to whisper in Winthrop's ear, all men who were members of the church – were allowed to elect the governor, the magistrates, and later representatives from each town. Following the election, however, they were to obey these leaders. On one occasion political rivals encouraged some church members to challenge Winthrop's actions as governor. When the effort at impeachment had failed, the governor gave a little speech: "Concerning liberty, I observe a great mistake in the country about that. There is a twofold liberty, natural (I mean as our nature is now, corrupt) and civil or federal [liberty]. The first is common to man with beasts and other creatures. By this man . . . hath liberty to do as he lists; it is a liberty to do evil as well as good. This liberty is inconsistent and incompatible with authority. The other kind of liberty [which] I call civil or federal, . . . is a liberty to do that only which is good and just and honest. This liberty is maintained and exercised in a way of subjection to authority. [As in marriage, where] the woman's own choice makes such a man her husband, yet being so chosen he is her lord; and a true wife accounts her subjection [to be] her honor and freedom and would not think her condition safe and free, but in subjection to her husband's authority. Even so, brethren, it will be between you and your magistrates." The response of the voters of Massachusetts Bay was to elect Winthrop governor again and again. Thus again commonality and hierarchy flowed into the most stable possible order, not only in Winthrop's mind but also in the wider convictions of his public. There is evidence that the men of New England also governed their towns on the same principles of election and subsequent obedience.

This political order acquired such a dimension in Winthrop's mind that it seemed at times a transcendent end in itself. To Winthrop, elections meant not only that "popular" men were elected, or that being elected they could expect to command popular support, but also that the very act of election unified electors and leaders in a holy compact of election, leadership, and support. United in this way, men would possess God's order. More humble versions of these concerns appear to have operated within the townships of New England. European peasants had long found that their deepest personal security, in terms of psychological satisfaction, in terms of protection from internal competitors, and in terms of defense against outside threats, lay in the unity of the group. And the surest unity was a consensus to which all could and did subscribe, a consensus sealed by a unanimous vote and expressed in laws and in leaders who were thereafter beyond question. The vote in such an instance was a symbolic testimony to a consensus already reached, and a pledge of obedience. This is most certainly how the local suffrage was used in the villages of New England. Regardless of laws which variously expanded and contracted the right to vote in town affairs, all towns generally let almost anyone speak in meeting. They permitted all but women, dependent sons, and servants to vote approval of the resulting consensus. Dissenting ballots were rare, however, for the bulk of votes were unanimous. Thereafter it was unthinkable to speak out against a decision or a leader, or to organize opposition within the village, much less to appeal to a higher authority. This happened, but it was accompanied by shocked expressions and protests, in defense of a unity and so of an order which had become virtually sacred. As it was in Winthrop's City Upon a Hill so it was in the villages scattered across the landscape of New England.

But Puritanism was more than patterns of civil authority. It was also a God awesome in his inscrutability, although somewhat revealed in his Word. The preachers of New England preached this God in the full wrath of his indignation, in the sureness of his ordained order of all things, and in the seductiveness of his grace. The people came, and listened, and paid the ministers well. A few carefully transcribed the sermons in their notebooks. Some agonized over telling phrases in their diaries. Often these were men and women well thought of in their communities.

Out of the ambiguities of an inscrutable God who somehow deigned to reveal his order and perhaps his salvation to men, burst a sudden obsession with a pure church. Here the way to God's order seemed clear. After generations of gathering devoted congregations amid the corruptions of England, it occurred to some ministers that churches of the elect were what God intended. In New England they began to declare that only "visible saints," persons probably received of God's grace, could be full members of a congregation. At moments their whole experiment seemed to depend on this point of doctrine. Churches accepted it, and all over the colony devout persons narrated the arrival of possible grace on their sinful souls. Many were heard and most were admitted to the congregations. So many churches endorsed the doctrine and so many persons offered themselves that among the first generation of settlers more than three-quarters of all households had a husband or a wife or both among the saints.

In the next generation the proportion who experienced divine grace dwindled, and so fewer men and women became church members. Men who did not experience grace and so did not become members were under the law not eligible to vote for the colony's leaders. Yet in 1665 hundreds of men thereby excluded from the church and from the vote signed petitions in support of the existing "Godly, righteous, and peaceable" order in Massachusetts. These men endorsed the idea of a church of saints even though its continuing high standards excluded them from religious and political fellowship. The belief in a pure church – and, one might add, in a pure state – was that enduring.

It is no contradiction that the moderate balancing of commonality and hierarchy in politics was followed by a runaway desire for a pure church. The common element was that each was a means to that perfect order which Puritanism sought. Even moderation, then, the political balancing, and the ambivalent God often reduced to a search for purity fully as intense as the pursuit of the perfect church. Nowhere is this better seen than in the histories of individual New Englanders. The Reverend Mr. Thomas Shepard was a moderate man who typically found the middle ground in his advice to his son, who was entering Harvard College: "Abhor therefore one hour of idleness as you would be ashamed of one hour of drunkenness [yet] order your studies [so as to] make them as pleasant as may be. Let not your studies be prosecuted in an immethodical or disorderly way [yet] let your studies be so ordered as to have [a] variety of

studies before you. Suffer not too much [time] to be
spent and broken away in visits, visiting or being visited, [yet] single out two or three scholars most godly,
learned, and studious whom you can most love and
who love you best, to be helps to you in your studies."
These counsels appear less avuncular when one con-
siders that an angry God lay on either side of the
golden mean. Be not idle, as "God will curse your
soul, while [this] sin is nourished." Yet do not work
unpleasantly long or hard, "so that you may not be
weary in the work God sets you about." As for the
mean itself, wise studying, "it is to fit you for the
most glorious work which God can call you to, the
holy ministry. Remember [also] the end of your life,
which is a coming back again to a God and fellowship
with God." For such Puritans, moderation was the
tightrope of purity.

Moderation in this respect was closely allied to
suppression of the self. Although Shepard walked the
rope with grace and dignity, others could be considerably more agitated by the effort to suppress every
stray impulse on either side of the right way. The
Reverend Michael Wigglesworth, after restraining
his impulses to the point of refusing intercourse with
his wife, would then become guilty over not perform-
ing as a dutiful husband. John Dane, tailor, got so
tired of wrestling with himself that "I bent myself to
New England, thinking that I should be more free
there than here from temptations." He was not. In

their struggles such people may have achieved God's external decency, but perhaps not always that union with God which was the goal of the Puritan personality. Sometimes, as with Michael Wigglesworth, they sought to reaffirm their personal purity by shutting other people's unlatched doors, banging in the wind.

❧

History entered the Puritans' garden through doors which neither Wigglesworth nor his compatriots could ever slam. Prosperity entered, and bits of the England they had fled. The violent reaction of villagers in Salem revealed that two New Englands had emerged from the tense balancings of the founders, one cosmopolitan and reconciled to the future, the other local and forever unreconciled.

By the 1640s, substantial merchants emerged to claim a share of power. They began to affect the elegancies of commercial magnates everywhere. Some elegance had been intended from the beginning and, especially as magistrates were sometimes merchants and merchants magistrates, the sumptuary laws permitted men in this double station to dress accordingly. What was remarkable was the growth of the mercantile affectation, its spread among the magistrates and ministers of the Bay, and the intensity of the local reaction to it.

In 1640 Mrs. William Hibbens, wife of a substantial Bostonian, commissioned an elaborate carved

27

chimneypiece and then a bed in the same "fashionable" style. She then accused the carpenter of over-
charging. Her recriminations so spread throughout
the community that a threat of excommunication
seemed the only way to silence her. Mrs. Hibbens was
a proud woman, and a quarrelsome one, and in the
ensuing trial she refused to humble herself. Peace was
at stake, and unity, so in the end the leaders of the
colony acting through the Reverend John Cotton had
no choice but to excommunicate her. This did not
alter her personality. Sixteen years later, then a wid-
ow, she was tried and executed as a witch. There is a
hint that Mrs. Hibbens was killed as much for her
pretensions as for her personality, and that the Renaissance was on trial again.

In more decorous fashion than Mrs. Hibbens the
merchants and the politicians of Massachusetts Bay
continued to commission carved elaboracies, and
soon they began to wear the ornate piled wigs of the
Restoration era. Cotton Mather, a surprisingly ornate man himself, defended periwigs early in 1691 in
a sermon on hypocrisy. "How wrong it is," said he,
"to be zealous against this innocent fashion, taken
up and used by the best of men, and yet make no
Conscience of being guilty of great Immoralities."
Replied Samuel Sewall, "I expected not to hear a
vindication of Periwigs in Boston Pulpit by Mr.
Mather."

From Salem came the rumblings of a minister who

*Cotton Mather, from an engraving by Peter Pelham 1727, courtesy of the American Antiquarian Society.*

would not countenance periwigs. Nicholas Noyes was to give a sermon entitled "Reasons against the Wearing of Periwigs, Especially against Men's Wearing of Periwigs Made of Women's Hair, as the Custom Now Is, Deduced from Scripture and Reason." What most immediately grated on Noyes was that a man in a periwig was in disguise, hence "strangely inconsistent with himself, and unlike today what he was like yesterday, and so less liable to be known." In fact periwigs were "used for disguise by the worst of men, as by shaven-crown popish priests, highway robbers, etc." Noyes went on to dwell on the deep "unnaturalness" of men who wore periwigs. The lecture was an open attack on the magistrates, several of whom were also merchants, and on the ministers who affected these devices. Lest his point be lost, he concluded: "Christians [are] especially grieved when they see magistrates and ministers, that are in reputation for wisdom, honor, and office, and ought to be examples to others in what is good, [but] are, in their opinion, become examples in what is evil."

Noyes's lecture reeked reminiscently of the complaints of Puritans a century before in England. There was no straitness of land in Massachusetts, yet commerce, prosperity, and the upper reaches of social hierarchy were reemerging in Salem and in Boston. Noyes may have been objecting to these developments when he cried that men were not being themselves but were hiding cutthroat selfishness, heresy, and social ambition in the curls of outrageous fashion. He urged instead a return to "order and honor," to efforts at "relieving the poor," and to "the worship of God."

Beneath the minister's urgings lay plainly a concern that poor but earnest parishioners would be left behind in a race for social and political distinction, but there also lay a terrible fear of himself. Whether or not Noyes was tempted by the wealth and power represented by periwigs, he was somewhat frightened of the sexual associations they evoked in his mind. His lecture echoes with hatred of "goatish" women who would degrade themselves "unto the rank and quality of a beast" by letting themselves be shorn to make periwigs for men. Oh, said Noyes, we might as well use all parts of women. "Their skins, well-tanned, may make good leather; and at length they will become very profitable creatures to men." He was also nervous about the homosexual overtones of periwigs: "And men, putting on their hair, have hair like women and not like men. It must needs be unlawful for men to desire it, and buy it, or beg it, to use in periwigs." This was the deepest "unnaturalness" of all. In trying to suppress periwigs, Noyes was suppressing not only the socially inevitable but also something of himself.

Noyes called on God and man to restore order to Massachusetts. He must have known that it was already too late. By 1691 the leaders of the colony were not only wearing periwigs but were also urging an accommodation with England, the source of periwigs, the place where such aristocratic social pretensions culminated in an increasingly centralized political power, and, to men like Noyes, the Antichrist itself.

In 1686 the crown had voided the colony's charter, which Winthrop had stretched into an independent constitution and Holy Covenant with God. Massachusetts was swept along with all the northern colonies into a royal Dominion of New England. The dominion's royal governor and council, the latter staffed by certain merchants and former magistrates, set out to integrate the Puritan colonies into the empire. A few councillors set out to enrich themselves in the process. Three years later the English revolution of 1688-9 provided an excuse to destroy the dominion. Mobs quickly imprisoned both governor and councillors, condemning them as appointees of the "papist" James II and joyfully acclaiming the accession of the Protestant William of Orange in England. Restoration of the charter, and so of purity, was expected imminently. But a new generation of accommodationists had emerged in control of the revolution in Boston. A Council of Safety largely made up of local merchants and led by Cotton and Increase Mather set out to negotiate a new charter with England. They knew that in the end there was no effective resistance to the forces of administrative centralization in England. Even the Protestant William would give Massachusetts just so much independence as a loyal English colony could expect. By 1691, the Mathers and company had obtained a charter which provided for a royal governor who, together with the elected representatives from the towns, would choose a council. The Puritan church would retain its support from the state but the Church of England would have to be allowed to preach, and worship, and build in Massachusetts.

Despite Noyes's opinions on periwigs, then, one of their chief defenders was busy trying to convince the people of the Bay that a charter which included a royal governor and envisioned an Anglican church in Boston was still sufficiently pure to constitute a new covenant with God. It is understandable that Noyes might have despaired of obtaining official support in his hatred of periwigs from an Establishment which had so given itself over to England.

It was at this point that everything fell out in Salem. It began early in 1692 with an adolescent girl, her imagination fired by sexual and personal resentments and focused by tales supplied by a black servant. To Noyes and the rural congregation of Salem village her claims of satanic affliction and their spread among her companions became a sign that something was terribly wrong. They had evidence enough that such corruptions as periwigs, and the commercial ambitions, social pretensions, and political aspirations which went with them, were already abroad in the neighboring port areas of Salem. These they knew were the work of the Devil. The Devil had led leaders in Salem and throughout the colony not only to wear periwigs, and to leave behind the simple life still led in the rural areas of Salem, but had also enticed them further to embrace a charter which would put the ruthless English aristocracy, their state, and their corrupt church in control of Massachusetts. It all smacked of conspiracy. That same Devil might strike down good people anywhere in his efforts to destroy God's own. It was not surprising, then, when innocent farm girls fell into seizures. Satan was completing his work in Massachusetts.

Oddly enough, the afflicted girls, subliminally encouraged by their audience, did not directly accuse the merchants of Salem or other leaders of the colony in Boston of being the instruments of Satan who had struck them down. At least initially, it was unthinkable for an adolescent girl to name such men as witches. Noyes's sermon on periwigs had been as bold as a minister's words dared be, and he had stopped with labeling the transgressors evil. Instead they picked vulnerable people – often local widows – natural targets for an insecure and resentful young girl. But an increasing number of the people accused as witches in Salem could also be linked to the premises and perils of periwiggery, even though they did not actually wear such appliances. Some were friends, or employees, or distant relatives, or political supporters of the emerging elite in the port of Salem. Others had striven for commercial success on their own, had failed, and had become the image of that failure which was the dark side of striving. Others, perhaps, had said a kind word for England. These were the persons who were accused as witches.

The invitation to the magistrates of the colony to sit in judgment was really a challenge. Would they continue to countenance evil, or would they come down squarely in favor of God's orthodoxy? The magistrates caved in; they accepted that witches must indeed be abroad in Salem, accepted the "spectral evidence" poured forth by the hysterical girls, and condemned a score of victims to death. Such distinguished men as Cotton Mather, William Stoughton, and Samuel Sewall sat on or advised the special court of Oyer and Terminer which heard the cases. Their orthodoxy in question, these leaders did not dare to do what a dozen previous judges in witchcraft cases had done, and send the accusers home. Half-persuaded of the righteousness of their actions, they dutifully hanged the chosen scapegoats.

The irony was thick, as the witches were in part surrogates for the "corruptions" of the judges themselves. There is an indication that Cotton Mather understood this and was willing to hang a few witches in order to purify their judges and win popular support for the new charter. The new royal governor,

Sir William Phips, who had arrived to initiate charter government just in time to appoint the special court at Salem, may have been a party to this game. Most of the judges were members of Mather's moderate procharter faction, and all by their very appointment became identified with the new regime. In a moment of confusion and uncertainty, some politicians may have been willing to pay a price in blood and in hypocrisy in order to assume more firmly the mantle of legitimacy.

Things went a bit too far, however, when the tormented girls moved their accusations closer to the villagers' real targets. Late in 1692 they attacked Lady Mary Phips, wife of the wealthy royal governor and a woman at the peak of the evolving social hierarchy in Massachusetts Bay. At this point ministers whose consciences had troubled them all along were heard in the appropriate places, and the trials were hastily shut down. It was not all hypocrisy. Five years later, provoked by strange dreams and by the death of an infant son, Samuel Sewall announced in a Boston church: "Samuel Sewall, sensible of the reiterated strokes of God upon himself and [his] family – and being [aware] that, as to the guilt contracted upon the opening of the late Commission of Oyer and Terminer in Salem, . . . he is upon many accounts more concerned than any he knows of – desires to take the blame and shame of it. Asking pardon of men and especially prayers that God . . . would pardon that sin and all his other sins . . . and that He would powerfully defend him against all temptations to sin for the future." Still, it was 1711 before the Royal Province of Massachusetts Bay reversed the convictions of the witches, and by then loyalty to the new charter was ensured.

Witchcraft never again troubled New England. Judges had learned it was a dangerous force. But the sources of the outbreak did not disappear. There remained in rural New England the confidence that here in America mankind lived as God intended, and that to the East something called corruption threatened. Corruption involved commerce, and competitive strivings, and dependency. It boiled up into a preoccupation with such fripperies as periwigs. It was horrible, and tempting. It was everything they had left England to avoid.

❧

A struggle long hidden within American Puritanism had revealed itself in the issues underlying the witchcraft accusations and trials, and it was not to be entirely suppressed until a new political individualism which it helped produce made it less relevant. Long before the migration to New England, Puritanism had begun to serve as a weapon in the hands of men and women who resented the erosion of local customs and local power by the evolving central state. These persons resisted, for example, the transfer of ancient local judicial and administrative powers from communal meetings or communally elected officials to self-perpetuating boards of gentlemen or to royally appointed justices of the peace. They complained over the transformation of elected local militia officers into officers appointed by the royal authorities. Their Puritanism was characterized by a passionate devotion to the authority of the local congregation. "Congregationalism" was their reply to an Anglican state church in which ministers appointed by bishops and bishops appointed by the king were increasingly tools in the hands of a royal state determined to centralize all authority, religious and secular, in its hands. By moving to New England, such men and women could hope to escape the tide of modernity engulfing them in the form of, among other things, a social hierarchy rising toward an ever more powerful and amoral central state. What they found there was a paradise. Townships and congregations seized power from a bewildered John Winthrop, who had dreamed of a single city on a hill but who could not resist the demands for autonomy from dozens of villages out in the forest.

The people of Salem Village had spoken out of this intensely localistic version of Puritanism. They held quite simply that God had intended men to live as they lived, and they reacted against corruptions which smacked not simply of a different life-style but also of a higher authority which would doom their life-style to extinction. Witchcraft was a desperate effort to ask whether the evolving social hierarchies culminating in the power of the central state were not in fact sinful. It was this localistic strain of Puritanism which had burst out in the witchcraft episode and which continued to compete for the allegiance of New Englanders.

The scandal of the witchcraft executions and the presence of an English governor, a royal council, and an Anglican church in Boston soon oriented the public face of Massachusetts toward the hierarchy of authorities culminating in the English crown. Men who had foregone the honor in Puritan days began to style themselves "gentlemen." Whether they opposed or aided the royal governor when elected to the lower house of the colonial legislature, these gentlemen enjoyed their association with a royal system of authority far more impressive in its way than the authority the colony could manage in Puritan days. Such men accepted commissions as royal justices of the peace in each county and began to increase the tax revenues flowing to this appointive level of government. A succession of wars with the French, beginning in 1690 and lasting until 1763, shifted still more authority and revenue farther upward from the towns, this time into the hands of the colonial government in Boston. That government now styled itself "the government of His Majesty's Province of Massachusetts Bay." The protests of the towns at this erosion of their power and at the evaporation of the purity of the days when a few saints in Boston had gingerly ruled them were barely heard. Yet in eighteenth-century Massachusetts as throughout New England a submerged localism continued to struggle against all higher authorities in the name of a persistent dream of local simplicity and local autonomy. The defenses of the localistic dream in the eighteenth century were ephemeral, hardly deserving the name of ideology. They often occurred only on the local level. When they did surface on the colonial level, they were often in the sphere of religion, as they had frequently been in seventeenth-century England. A generalized political resistance was as yet unthinkable. Yet the dream of religious piety, community, and autonomy had always been an integral part of a localism which also had political dimensions. Furthermore, the political implications of localism were never far below the surface.

The only ideologue of localism, if he could be called that, was the immensely popular Reverend John Wise. A spectacular athlete in his youth, Wise became the voice of resistance to higher authorities. Significantly, he confined his sentiments to the realm of religious debate, because explicit political localism had overtones of resistance to the English crown. Still, in 1717, twenty-five years after witchcraft, this respected minister offered a defense of New England's local "democracy" which was implicitly critical not only of the idea of hierarchical authority but of the

English monarchy itself. In his "Vindication of the Government of New England Churches," Wise extolled "a democracy, which is when sovereign power is lodged in a council consisting of all the members, and where every member has the privilege of a vote. This form of government appears in the greatest part of the world to have been the most ancient. For that reason seems to shew it to be most probable, that when men (being originally in a condition of natural freedom and equality) had thoughts of joining in a civil body, [they] would without question be inclined to administer their common affairs, by their common judgment, and so must necessarily to gratify that inclination establish a democracy . . . And moreover it seems very manifest that most civil communities arose at first from the union of families, that were nearly allied in race and blood. And though ancient stories make frequent mention of kings, yet it appears that most of them were such that had an influence rather in persuading, than in any power of commanding." Nominally Wise defended congregationalism against the advocates of Presbyterian church government, in which synods of elders and of priests would exercise central authority over the churches of a region. But in his view, synods were only the first step in a hierarchy of authorities which would culminate one day in an official state church which, like the English state itself, would be ruled by a few men and have the king at its head. By this time English authority over Massachusetts was so well established that Wise could not criticize openly the English crown. What he did instead was to praise to the skies the ancientness, reasonableness, and holiness of communal democracy, whether in the church or in civil life, and leave the listeners to draw their own conclusions about all other forms of government, church or civil. He observed merely, "It is *said* of the British Empire, that it is mixed monarchy, as that by the necessary concurrence of the Lords and Commons hath the main advantages both of a [Monarchy] Aristocracy, and of a Democracy."

Wise's praise of a nearly tribal localism and his skepticism of higher forms of authority were echoed viscerally in the actions of thousands of New Englanders in the eighteenth century. As time went on, town after town grew too large and their populations became too geographically scattered to easily meet or to reach a consensus on such vital issues as the location of roads or of the meetinghouse. Groups of "outlivers" then petitioned the selectmen of their towns for permission to secede. They wished to form new towns on the periphery of the old ones. Officially their reason was convenience. In their petitions for "separation" they cited the insuperable difficulty of wading through seas of snow to attend the church or town meetings usually held in the old center of town. These outlivers also hoped, by obtaining their own church and town meetings, to be better able to entice new settlers to join them and so to raise the value of their lands. But in many cases deeper reasons revealed themselves in the heat of the ensuing debates over the proposed secessions.

The people living in the centers of the overgrown towns fought these petitions for secession, arguing that the petitioners were poor people trying to escape taxes, or religious separatists seeking a minister more amenable to their notions, or persons with an intolerant obsession with "independency." Much of this was true. The outlivers were often reacting to the increasing social hierarchy, formalistic established religion, and elitist politics of the old center of town by seeking to establish a new town exclusively occupied by people such as themselves. Often they were subsistence farmers with a desire for a more intensely unifying religious experience and for a political leadership closely identified with their interests. They were seeking to remedy a violated sense of communal homogeneity by re-creating an intensely local authority in their section of the old town. As one group put it, in a rare slip which revealed their intentions, "We desire to be a free people of ourselves."

Outlivers' attitudes toward the county courts and provincial government were peculiar: If higher authorities would force the old town to grant them independence, such authorities would be accepted. Otherwise the petitioners would take matters into their own hands by seceding. Occasionally they burned the old meetinghouse, and they always built their own, leaving the civil and religious authorities to recognize the new reality. Their desire "to be a free people of ourselves" was seldom thwarted for long. Freedom and localism came together out in the New England countryside as many thousands of outlivers formed their "societies" and were recognized. This was what many New Englanders meant by "freedom": the right to secede into their own little worlds.

John Wise would be echoed again in the visceral localism of the Great Awakening. This religious revival of the 1740s is usually thought of as an evangelical movement which called upon the individual once again to find his own faith and through it to receive the saving grace of God in a transforming conversion experience graphically described as "rebirth." The tumults roused by fiery revivalist preachers not only created reborn individuals but also tore apart peaceful villages into awakened and unawakened factions, creating a lasting diversity of religious persuasions. It may have seemed only a short glance forward from these experiences to an America of independent individualists, each secure in his own religious and political faith and able to choose among a variety of such faiths. Yet individualism and diversity were not the immediate lessons of the Great Awakening in New England or elsewhere in the colonies.

In its deepest meaning the Awakening was also a

rebirth of the localistic impulse. The message that a vital faith was the sole standard of human quality leveled all social pretensions. Established ministers with college degrees, ministers who wore, yes, even periwigs, found that their religious authority had fallen in the dust. Neither they nor the official "consociations" and synods and state churches which stood behind them had authority in the face of this leveling faith. What arose in their place was not the independent individual. It was the "we" of thousands of petitions for religious independence from groups of leveled individuals. Groups of such individuals united by their common inner experience formed "societies." They rejected the tired verities of established religion and asked for permission to take over the old church buildings or to forego taxes to the established church in their towns in order to build new, free churches. When permission was denied by the existing church or by the higher authorities of church and state, these societies seceded anyway. They ruled themselves, and did not live by the standards of scholars, priests, or gentlemen, or necessarily even by those of their own revivalist ministers, whom they easily dispensed with when displeased. Rather, they ruled by the moral authority of their common faith, and their records abounded with the strictest moral discipline. These congregations were often known at first as "Separates." Their action in separating paralleled what groups of outlivers had done

44

for decades; they separated in order to seek unified moral order with close control of a leadership which spoke to their needs. In this instance the explicit need was for a vital religion free of subjection to higher authorities. In a significant number of cases the out-livers and the awakened were the same.

The Great Awakening, because it was a colonial and an intercolonial phenomenon, raised such local-istic principles to a level where they could no longer be ignored. The implicit political statement which religious separations made was not ignored by the critics of the Awakening. Such skeptics as Charles Chauncy criticized the revival for its emotionalism and antiintellectualism, and also observed that sep-aration from established standards of religion and from the higher churchly and civil authorities which imposed these standards on localities "shook the foundations of the state." Critics could not conceive of a social order which did not involve an educated ministerial elite, armed with the powers of an official church and of the state, setting religious, moral, and political standards for the people. A community of revived individuals holding moral authority from God evoked visions of the Anabaptist reign in the German city of Munster in the sixteenth century, when a local sect had gained control of the town, given license to wild sexual orgies, and created whole-sale political chaos. No sensible state could tolerate such disorder in its midst. Yet the seeds of an intensely localistic moral order were there, in the Separates of the Awakening. The Separates' rejection of the power of higher political authorities to enforce a state religion on all was, as the critics suggested, a step toward a rejection of the power of political authorities in worldly affairs as well. In Connecticut, in fact, awakened communities took the next step when they challenged the schemes of established politicians in Hartford to gain control of the colony's western lands.

By the mid-eighteenth century it was only a question of time until the struggle between this native localism and the emerging hierarchies of authority on the provincial level became explicitly political. Suspicion of higher (and not simply of English) authorities had already begun to take an openly political form in the years immediately following the witchcraft trials. The abundance of land and a right to vote tied to the possession of land had sustained a superorthodox "popular" political movement which, under two Elisha Cookes, father and son, had sought to bend the new charter government back as far as possible toward the old Puritan ways. The people had wanted very much to be left alone in their villages and under God's law. In one sense this "popular" faction had merely championed in the political sphere that same godly, localistic democracy which Wise and the Great Awakening later sought to revive in the religious realm. In another sense the idea of an openly political

reaction against the building layers of higher authority was totally outside accepted forms of behavior.
Where might it lead?

The answer came in 1776, with the American Revolution. The Revolution invited all men to speak
their minds on the governance of the new American
states and so opened a Pandora's box which revealed
for the first time the full dimensions of that localism
long ago implicit within the witchcraft episode. During the Revolution, New England localists, bound by
tradition to an intense piety, their piety renewed in
the Great Awakening, discovered that getting rid of
the king had not gotten rid of religious formalism,
of social "aristocracy," or of governmental centralization. When the question arose of what sort of constitution to write for the new state of Massachusetts,
they began a political contest for men's souls unprecedented in its explicitness. Tom Paine, son of an
English dissenting minister, became the ideologue of
the localists. Paine had extolled the little group of
men governing themselves "under the Oak Tree."
He suggested that "to the degree government departs
from this authority, government is wrong." The
Massachusetts town of Ashfield put it more bluntly:
"We desire to have no governair but the guvernair of
the univarse." God, local men, and local power were
enough for Ashfield.

Political issues now dominated. In a haunting twist
of history, a number of towns in western and in

47

southeastern Massachusetts requested that, regardless of whatever authority might be left in the hands of county and of state governments by any state constitution, the registration of land titles, the probate of estates, and the election of militia officers be placed back in local hands. In some cases all the judicial functions of the once centrally appointed county court justices were to be moved back into the control of the towns. These demands were a literal re-creation of local demands in sixteenth-century England. Beneath the surface of eighteenth-century New England life an ancient political localism had remained alive. Hysterical in the witchcraft accusations, hidden between the lines of petitions for new towns, and largely confined to the realm of religion, as in John Wise and in the Separate congregations of the Awakening, localism had nonetheless persisted. With the Revolution, it stepped forward to raise the most basic issues of political control, more powerfully than had ever been the case in old England.

Political hierarchs such as John Adams shrank from the idea that a localistic mentality could be a basis for a functioning government. The delegation of authority to aristocratic leaders was to these sophisticates a precondition of a valid state. The struggle between an overtly political localism and the domestic version of hierarchy cultivated by such men as Adams, a struggle partially obscured by other interests, raged back and forth in the contest over the

framing of a state constitution in the newly independent Massachusetts. By 1780 the hierarchs had won
a constitution which featured extensive delegation of
authority to the state, only to face renewed and now
armed local resistance seven years later from Daniel
Shays and his followers in the villages of western
Massachusetts. Later, many Massachusetts localists
joined some state politicians to resist the imposition
of still another layer of higher authority in the form
of the federal Constitution. In the end neither localism nor "aristocratic" hierarchy retained the exact
form sketched out in the witchcraft era, when local
virtue had so subtly resisted the higher pretensions
symbolized by periwigs and by an English governor.
But demonstrably the marvelously balanced unities
of the Puritans had given way to two contending
views of the political universe, neither of which had
gained mastery over the populace of New England.

ॐ

The localism revealed in the history of Massachusetts
took various forms. It was an English tradition of
local resistance to the emerging national state. It
was the congregationalism which was the religious
expression of that tradition. It was rural Salem, mad
with the thought of periwigged hierarchs in commerce, in the pulpits, and in politics, their curled
heads nodding approval of a governor sent out by the
English Antichrist. It was the avid fastening upon of
the support seemingly given by such rare intellectuals

as John Wise (and, later, Tom Paine). It was a hundred groups of outlivers petitioning to separate from old towns and churches in order to be "a free people." It was the religious Separates of the Great Awakening. It was, finally, the resolve to have no governor but God, which was an impulse openly offered as a program by small townships of backwoods Massachusetts during the American Revolution. Yet it was a single phenomenon. Everywhere the impulse was to level the community by placing the supreme value on membership in the community and to make local leadership, political or religious, responsible to this community and to its values. Elites, and ministers, were accepted as long as they were legitimized locally rather than by their higher allegiances. The consistent enemy was the tendency of such elites to become part of a self-legitimizing Anglo-American gentry which, with its attendant ministry, verified its own superiority by self-reflection in an endless set of hierarchical social mirrors. This elite both legitimized and, further, was legitimized by a hierarchy of often appointive offices leading up first to the English crown, and later, to the American nation-state. This elite, and its state, increasingly left no room for local control.

Localism arose strengthened from the conditions of life in seventeenth- and even to a degree in eighteenth-century New England. Many men still lived far from sophisticated commerce, away from true gentlemen, elusively distant from the authority of appointed justices, tax collectors, land registrars, and from bishops, synods, and ministerial consociations. (Even until the middle of the eighteenth century, John Adams's well-to-do farmer father had called himself a yeoman.) In so many towns a locally validated elite had served mainly to protect local custom from a government which had asked little and offered less. "Localism" simply asked that this isolation continue. Yet, although deeply descriptive of the conditions of American life, localism failed to express itself as a creative ideology. It was too visceral, too much in the realm of the uneducated. No real intellectual could associate it with anything save the Anabaptists, the Levellers, the Diggers, and all the wild sects of the Protestant Reformation. True, the secessions of localism were hastening New England toward a day when contention in society would be the norm, and when a diversity of religious and political views would exist. When that day came, not just groups but also individuals would feel free to contend for the liberty to select among a diversity of persuasions. The individual's right to contend and to select would become a sacred part of his right to self-realization. Thus, individualism would become the ultimate localism, and would have an ideology of its own. But localists would have been horrified by a future so far from their communal vision.

Their hierarchical superiors fared no better, for

precisely opposite reasons. These "gentlemen" were marvelously articulate. Armed with two centuries of European political ideology, they manipulated confidently the scenery of the modern state. But the Mathers, Phipses, Chauncys, and Adamses of New England scrambled without success to maintain deference to their social position and to the authority of the states in which they participated, for they were not securely based in American circumstance. Such men struggled eternally to make prevail a hierarchical principle of legitimacy which did not fit a large part of the American experience. By the time of the American Revolution their counterparts in other colonies faced the same dilemma.

# Colonial Virginia

JOHN Smith was a natural man, even a natural gentleman. The son of uncertain parentage, he fought his way through obscure Transylvanian wars to the title of captain. Home, worn, and wounded at the age of twenty-five, he faced the prospect of subservient posturings until he might enter the service of some lord, and so serve out his life. Typically, he sailed instead for Virginia. At first he hoped only for another war, believing that Indians must be easier than Turks. He found his war, and a new land, Virginia, which stunned his imagination and opened his hopes. Smith threw himself into his new land. His writings demanded that Englishmen sit up and listen, and far transcended the usual promotional literature.

"We chanced upon a land," wrote Smith, "even as God made it," echoing the phrase of an earlier explorer in an exclamation which would haunt Americans in generations to come. Whether Virginia or New England, it did not matter to Smith. It was all a natural land where a man might be himself: "Who can desire more content than to tread and plant that ground he hath purchased by hazard of his life? If he have but the taste of virtue and magnanimity, what can be more pleasant than planting and building a foundation for his posterity, gotten from the rude earth by God's blessing and his own industry?"

To live in America instead of in England, Smith elaborated, "is the difference between the use of arms in the field and on the monuments of stones, [between] the golden age and the leaden age, prosperity and misery, justice and corruption, substance and shadows, experience and [mere] imagination, making commonwealths, and marring commonwealths, the fruits of virtue and the conclusions of vice." Who could stand at home idly when the world had such a life to offer?

It was more than prosperity which Smith saw and more than justice or even creativity. This was finally a world in which a man might be ennobled: "What more truly suits with honor and honesty, as the discovering [of] things unknown, erecting towns, peopling countries, informing the ignorant, reforming things unjust, teaching virtue . . . For gentlemen, what exercise should more delight them than ranging daily these unknown parts, using fowling and fishing, for hunting and hawking. See you not a hawk?"

Chafing under the polite viciousness of organized society, Smith had longed for this land all of his life. The hawk was Smith himself, or that last, wild nobility to which men must respond. It was the hawk, too, of Robinson Jeffers, another free spirit in a stifling age:

A falcon has perched.
I think, here is your emblem
To hang in the future sky;
Not the cross, not the hive,
But this; bright power, dark peace . . . .

You do not know him, you communal people;
Intemperate and savage,
Beautiful and wild.*

New England soon succumbed to the "absolute crew, only of the elect," leaving Smith to seek a renewed role in Virginia. That colony was plagued by an oversupply of "natural" men fully as ambitious as Smith but less visionary. They had routed him from the governorship in 1609, and their subsequent troubles were exacerbated by an Indian attack in 1622, which left the colony totally disorganized. Now, in 1624, they rejected Smith again, and he had to surrender Virginia in turn to the vicissitudes of history: "But here I must leave all to the trial of time, both myself, [and] Virginia's preparations, proceedings, and good events, praying to that great God the protector of all goodness to send them as good success as the goodness of the action and country deserveth and my heart desireth."

❦      ❦      ❦

* From "Rock and Hawk," p. 792, and "Hurt Hawk," pp. 789, 790, F. O. Matthiessen, ed., *Oxford Book of American Verse* (1950, Oxford University Press, rpt. 1958).

PRAYERS NOTWITHSTANDING Virginia must have often seemed a Hobbesian nightmare. Or worse, for Hobbes's natural men fled from a "solitary, poor, nasty, brutish and short" life into the refuge of strong government, an act that was beyond the capacities of seventeenth-century Virginians.

The troubles had begun already in Smith's time, when hunger, fear, and frustration gave spur to every would-be gentleman's ambitions. In the summer of 1607 Captain Newport advised the president of the colony's council, Edward Maria Wingfield, of impending danger: Captain Gosnold "was strong with friends and followers, and could [depose the president] if he would," while Mr. Archer "was troubled by an ambitious spirit." Captain Newport then left for England to seek provisions.

By August there were only six able-bodied but hungry men left to put up a defense against the Indians. Forty men had died, among them the "worthy and religious" Gosnold, who had in fact proven loyal. Mr. Kendall, a friend of Mr. Archer, then made the first move against Wingfield. Kendall was promptly removed from the council and imprisoned for "practicing to sow discord between President and Council." Some of the remaining councillors immediately demanded "a larger allowance [of corn] for themselves and for some sick [persons] their favorites – which the President would not yield unto." Finally, on September 10, 1607, Councillors Ratcliffe, Martin, and John Smith "came to the President with a warrant subscribed under their hands to depose the President." This they did, making Ratcliffe president in the face of a silent majority of the council, which took no side in the events.

Mr. Archer, whom Wingfield considered the "ringleader," had stayed safely out of sight, but soon emerged as recorder or secretary of a rearranged council. Whereupon Edward Maria Wingfield was put to trial and found guilty of, among other things, denying one man "a penny-whistle, a chicken, a spoonful of beer, and serving him foul corn." Wingfield was imprisoned in a pinnace offshore.

John Smith, looking back on these events, was hard put to justify them. He remarked philosophically that "such actions have ever since the world's beginning been subject to such accidents [as befell Wingfield] and everything of worth is found full of difficulties; but nothing [is] so difficult as to establish a commonwealth so far remote from men and means and when men's minds are so untoward as neither do well themselves or suffer others." It is hard to tell whether this is an indictment of Wingfield or of the conspirators. Smith admitted that "the new President and Martin [were] little beloved [and] of weak judgment in dangers and less industry in peace." Their only virtue, apparently, was that they "committed the management of all things abroad" to Captain Smith, who "by his own good example" set a few things right.

Despite Smith the conspiracy soon darkened into murder. A blacksmith was condemned to be hanged for striking Mr. Archer. To save his own life he accused the now-released Kendall of plotting a mutiny against the mutineers. Kendall was immediately shot to death. Wingfield, who had witnessed the execution from the pinnace, now shouted across the water that he would expose the whole sordid business once he returned to England. Friends of the conspirators shot at him, missed, and there followed a long parley concerning who was the true president, who the true councillors, and who was possessed of the legitimate authority in the colony. No one seemed to know. The confusion had been compounded when Kendall had claimed, just before his death, that the new President Ratcliffe was really a villain named Sicklemore.

Wingfield now lived in fear for his life, "praying God they did not think of any ill thing unworthy of themselves." When Smith left on an expedition, Archer "began to call Mr. Smith's life into question." Smith would have had his trial on the day of his return and his hanging the same or the next day had not the arrival of Captain Newport stopped all executions. Newport fed everyone, packed Wingfield and Archer off to England, and order of a sort was restored to Virginia.

But Smith went off exploring again, Newport went home to England, and the English camp fell into renewed starvation, disorder, and scheming. Smith himself came and went as governor of the would-be colony, to be succeeded by others of equal power and in the end uncertain authority. Not just in the starving times but throughout the seventeenth century Virginia continued to be characterized by a desperate tragicomedy of power struggles and by a society not only disorderly but also uncertain to its very core. While Hobbes's men escaped into a strong state, seventeenth-century Virginians remained transfixed as "on a darkling plain, swept with confused alarms of struggle and flight, where ignorant armies clash by night."

Government by the Virginia Company collapsed into direct royal control in 1624. The king's governors fared little better than the leaders sent out by the company. Governor Sir John Harvey was undone by ambitious councillors who used every excuse to stir the colonists against him. They hinted that he was a papist, a lover of Indians, a tyrant. Harvey realized that the opposition was chiefly a matter of councillors eager for more power and patronage, but could not understand the whirlwind of accusations which culminated in his recall by the king in 1639. Harvey sailed bewildered back to England, to be replaced by a far more knowing Sir William Berkeley. With an interruption during the Puritan Revolution in England, from 1652 to 1660, after the revolutionary Parliament had sent a military expedition which compelled Virginians to set aside their royalist governor, Berkeley remained in office until 1676. Yet even Berkeley met his schemers, led by Nathaniel Bacon and backed by a new wave of popular alarm over Indian incursions and governmental abuses. Their rebellion failed, but Berkeley in turn was recalled.

Never were armies more ignorant or the plain darker than during Bacon's Rebellion. Confused slaughters by Indians and by whites, troops nominally attacking Indians and in truth levering Berkeley out of Jamestown, truces and pardons and bluffs, midnight flights by Bacon and Berkeley and then again by Bacon, succeeded one another with bewildering frequency. In this tangle of legitimacies Bacon was alternately a royal councillor, an ad hoc Indian fighter, a rebel against Berkeley, a general for the colony against the Indians, a member of the House of Burgesses, again a rebel, and finally dead of a bloody flux in the midst of his rebellion. In the confusion many men, white and red, died. The result was merely a new royal governor.

So it went, throughout the early South. In Maryland and the Carolinas, too, governors came and went and schemers became councillors and councillors schemers until no man knew where authority lay. Local "magnates" pulled the cloak of authority indiscriminately about themselves and ruled, or tried to, in its name. Only a novelist could render the mystery of it all, and a novelist has. The best way to understand seventeenth-century Maryland is to read *The Sot-Weed Factor*, by John Barth. Barth set out to write a history and had to write a novel. The central figure in the story is the enigmatic John Coode, an actual figure, who appears and disappears in a dozen disguises and skulking rebellions against the governors of the Catholic proprietors, the lords of Baltimore. In 1688 the Glorious Revolution in England gave Coode his chance, and he succeeded briefly in seizing power in the name of an earnest Protestantism. Once in power he mysteriously melted away and was never seen again, like the snows which sometimes fall on these parts of Maryland.

The absurdity of such figures was not so great as first meets the eye. In the 1720s, at a relatively early stage in the history of North Carolina, the usual processes of disorder unseated a man named George Burrington from his post as proprietary governor. On November 15, 1725, a drunken Burrington swaggered around to the house of Thomas Parris, a political ally to the new governor, Sir Richard Everard, and in the three-o'clock darkness pounded on the door. When Burrington was let in, he rushed into the sickroom of another Everard man, Adam Cockburn, collector of His Majesty's customs in Rappahinnock in Virginia, crying "Are all you country men such fools as Sir Richard Everard?" and threatening to cut off the somnolent Cockburn's ears. Burrington swore that within nine months he would be governor again, and would restore his followers to the lucrative offices in the region. With a drink and an oath to cut off the ears of Sir Richard Everard, he disappeared into the night. A few weeks later, fortified once again by drink, Burrington made it all the way to Everard's house in the company of some "ruffians." He shouted to the new governor: "Come out. I want satisfaction of you for saying you would send me to England in irons. Therefore come out and give it me, you Everard, you a Knight, you a Baronet, you a Governor. You are a Sancho Panza and I'll take care of you, you numskull head." The literary but besotted Mr. Burrington then staggered away. By 1731 Burrington and friends had created enough stir to discredit not only Everard but proprietary government in general, and George Burrington became the first royal governor of North Carolina – briefly.

Under the assaults of Archers, Bacons, Coodes, and Burringtons, Southern governments could not stand. They came and went as "reasons" and "justifications" floated back and forth to a bemused England. If a governor represented a lordly proprietor in England, and above all if that proprietor were Catholic, his authority was minimal at the start. Self-made and not disinterested "captains" would lead the inhabitants in a plea for a royal and safely Protestant governor. This ploy succeeded, temporarily, in Maryland, and similar attacks destroyed proprietary rule in the Carolinas. When the governor was royal he might still be branded "Catholic" but the more generalized cry of "despot" was also reliable, as it had proven earlier against Governor Harvey in Virginia. Removed from the panoply which made them eminences in England, these royal governors, knights and baronets included, were easily sacrificed to the fears of the inhabitants. England was never sure what had happened, so the governor was usually called home and replaced.

The hilarious and sometimes deadly disrespect shown by real and feigned leaders toward one another was naturally also shown by the lower orders of society toward those contending for power above them. In spite of their efforts to unseat proprietary and royal governors, the self-made "captains" of the local scene often received the most coruscating criticisms. Ebeneezer Cooke, a lad of common origins but poetic aspirations, came to Maryland late in the seventeenth century. Shocked at finding no gentry worthy of patronizing his doggerel, he wrote the original "Sot-Weed Factor" in revenge against the pretensions of the Maryland planters. His description of a county court is beyond comment:

> We sat like others, on the ground,
> Carousing punch in open air,
> Till cryer did the Court declare:

The planting rabble being met,
Their drunken worships likewise sat;
Cryer proclaims that noise should cease,
And straight the Lawyers broke the peace,
Wrangling for plaintiff and defendant,
I thought they would never make an end on it.
With nonsense, stuff, and false quotations,
With brazen lies, and allegations;
And in the splitting of the cause
They used such motions with their paws
As showed their zeal was strongly bent
In blows to end the argument.
A reverend Judge, who to the shame
Of all the Bench, could write his name,
At [a] petty-fogger took offence,
And wondered at his impudence.
The Bench in fury straight divide,
And scribes take on the Judge's side;
The Jury, Lawyers, and their Clients,
Contending, fight, like earth-born giants.
The Court adjourned in usual manner,
In battle, blood, and fractious clamour.

Anne, the wife of one William Fowler of Virginia, expressed this contempt even better: "The Deposition of Gilbert Guy, age 28 years or thereabouts, sworn and examined, sayeth that, being at the house of William Fowler, discoursing with him concerning certain casks found by the servant of Captain Adam

Thorougood [a Justice of the Peace] by the seaside but afterwards seized and taken away by the aforesaid William Fowler, the aforesaid deponent told him it would vex [Thorougood] to have the said casks taken away from him. Thereupon the wife of the said William Fowler asked who would take them from him [Fowler]. The said deponent answered, 'Captain Thorougood,' upon which she the said Anne Fowler answered, 'Let Captain Thorougood kiss my arse.' "

The turbulent freemen were not alone in their contempt. In Virginia and in Maryland from ten to thirty persons in every hundred were servants who had sold themselves into terms of labor in order to pay for their passages to America. They labored for terms of four to seven years, usually in the tobacco fields. Such servants were least likely of all to respect drunken masters who were often themselves former servants. Such masters, above all in their continual challenging of the legitimacy of the governors above them, did not engender a respectful submission in their servants. Some servants fought, and others voted with their feet, but whether they fought or ran they were usually apprehended and punished with added years of labor. In this way voluntary servants became involuntary convicts working under hated masters on extended terms. At its bottom, the Southern society of the seventeenth century culminated in a convict population as dangerous as that of nineteenth-century Australia.

The captains and embryonic gentlemen realized, as they struggled for power, what problems they faced beneath themselves. They could do nothing. Tobacco demanded servants to labor in the fields. Servants ran away and were convicted or finished their terms free, disrespectful, and poor. The dilemma was poignantly revealed in a letter to the king and Privy Council in England, explaining why Virginia had not mounted a better defense against a Dutch raid on the tobacco fleet as it lay offshore in July, 1673. "Virginia [they explained] is intersected by so many vast rivers as makes more miles to defend than we have men of trust to defend them. For by our nearest computation we leave at our backs as many servants (besides Negroes) as there are freemen to defend the shores and all our frontiers [against] the Indians. Both [of] which give men fearful apprehensions of the danger they leave their estates and families in, whilst they are drawn from their houses to defend the borders. Of which number [of freemen, moreover] also at least one third are single freemen whose labor will hardly maintain them, or men much in debt, both of which we may reasonably expect, upon any small advantage the enemy may gain upon us, would revolt [and join the enemy] in hopes of bettering their condition by sharing the plunder of the country with them."

❧

Smith's dream had come to naught, and the reasons why are fairly clear. The South had got too many "natural" men in a natural situation much like that envisioned by political philosophers. What the philosophers forgot to narrate was the difficulty of forming a legitimate state under excessively "natural" conditions.

There was a surplus of single men, for as late as 1700 there were three men to every two women in the South. These men had come here to rise, which in the heady atmosphere of a New World seemed deceptively easy. None lightly brooked interference. Yet as tobacco prices leveled off or, in some colonies, as no staple crop emerged, and as a few men engrossed land and power, mere existence became as much as the remnant could expect. It was an existence without marriage and without ready means to the success which others enjoyed.

In Virginia and in Maryland tobacco agitated the men who seemed to have been successful. Especially in times of falling prices, tobacco created a hunger for more land and more labor which when satisfied only exacerbated the emerging divisions in the society. The alternate response to falling prices was to restrict the import of servants and slaves and to diversify crops in order to break the deadly cycle of cash-crop dependency. But when governors tried this policy they met with violent opposition from the body of planters. Yet at other times planter associations took an opposite tack and, when the government refused to limit tobacco production as a device to raise prices, their members went about destroying plants and threatening reluctant planters. Under such conditions it was no source of stability that most men had the vote. What ambition dictated the suffrage seemed to sanction, and politics within as without the suffrage often became a chaotic seeking.

England, which should have been a source of stability, merely increased the uncertainty; appeals there depended on the winds of a still uncertain politics. Sometimes these winds blew a governor out of office, as when the Puritan Revolution took away Berkeley in the 1650s. Other times they wafted to the colonies the uncertain influences of an emerging Imperial policy, most notably the Navigation Acts of the subsequent decades. On still other occasions changes in England excited wholesale revolt, one case being the use of the Glorious Revolution by Protestant planters in Maryland as an excuse to throw off the hated Catholic proprietors.

Disorder was the not too surprising result of such conditions. Not that this was a more violent society than others of its time – it was not. No more men were killed in Bacon's Rebellion than in the Pequot War, or in Salem in the calmer confines of New England. Burrington's bluster seems almost charming beside the deadly intensities of the New Englanders. Conversely, New England had its share of bluster, too, for magistrates cursed each other and there too the lower orders offered arses to be kissed by their putative superiors. Yet in the seventeenth-century South the sum total of ribaldry, rebellion, and open resentment was if not a violence then certainly a disorder not found elsewhere.

One solution was the law. The remarkable thing about the seventeenth-century South was the pervasiveness of the law. Consider that most of the evidence of disorder comes from legal documents. The rebel Archer had himself appointed secretary to the Virginia Council, where he recorded his inequities in correct legal form. Burrington's blunderings were preserved in the depositions of a formal trial. The absurdities Ebeneezer Cooke loved most occurred in the course of a county court. Mrs. Fowler paid for her "kiss my arse" to Mr. Justice Thorougood with twenty lashes and an apology. This apology is significant, as it was no mere coercion which the law undertook; subtle forms of punishment were used as well, most notably the public shaming of the offender so often employed elsewhere. Mrs. Fowler was ordered "to ask forgiveness of the said Captain Thorougood here [in court] and also the ensuing Sunday at Linhaven [Church]." In another case Joan Butler, having called the wife of Edward Drew "a common cunted whore," was ordered to be keelhauled, caned, or to "present herself before the minister at the time of divine service and say after him [that] I Joan Butler do acknowledge to have called Marie Drew 'whore' and thereby confess I have done her manifest wrong wherefore I desire before this congregation that the said Marie Drew will forgive me and also that this congregation will join and pray with me that God may forgive me." In a final instance, Michael Fletcher "[having] fraudulently taken tobacco out of several casks and in the room thereof put in bad tobacco [was] ordered committed to the sheriffs custody until such time as he stand at the court door for one hour with a paper in his hat written in capital letters, 'Behold and beware by my example how ye cheat and abuse tobacco.' "

In spite of these legal efforts the evidences of disorder high and low persisted in Southern society. The law alone was not enough, for beneath disorder and arising from the same social sources as disorder lay a corrosive lack of legitimacy which ate away at every effort to establish a legal order. Legitimacy might be defined as the willingness to accept some person, principle, or institution as a basis for the exercise of authority. There was little such willingness in the seventeenth-century South. If Sir Richard Everard, Baronet, did not evoke legitimacy, neither did a Burrington, and still less a Ratcliffe-Sicklemore or a disappearing Coode. Only the frank good sense of a Captain Newport, a real sea-captain, carried with it the coin of legitimacy – and that was small coin. Chaotic individualism had bred not only disorder, then, but also this final corrosion. Skepticism's monument was Ebeneezer Cooke's pitiful image of clients, lawyers, scribes, and judges, none accepting the others' legitimacy or the legitimacy of the principles behind the court, flailing at one another in continuing disorder.

The result was the failure of the law and, above it, the failure of all higher principles of political legitimacy. Amidst these failures the populace had nowhere to turn for leadership. Made conscious of the defects even of royal minions by their ambitious "betters," the people were also conscious that these men constituted no better principle of legitimacy. When the instabilities of their situation – whether too many taxes, low prices, or an Indian threat – moved the inhabitants to seek leadership, they could only turn to men whose legitimacy they could not finally accept. Mere disorder became a volatile search for a true leader. Voters and servants for a time eagerly pursued every Archer, Coode, Bacon, or Burrington who promised to establish what could not be established in such a society, a legitimate political order. The result was that civil and political society struggled without success for a coherent existence.

෴

Sir William Berkeley strode onstage as the master of all Virginia's problems. And for thirty years he was. Berkeley understood that the first need was for legitimacy. If Virginians believed in him and in the principles he represented, then they would obey his supporters and his law and there would be order. Berkeley set out like a Tudor monarch to evoke that faith

71

which gave legitimacy. Or rather, he set out more like an artist, and at times he was the leader of a glorious renaissance masque straight from the court of the Stuart kings. This is no conceit, for the young cavalier had once affected himself a playwright. The piece he created would have won the praise of John Smith, it contained roles for all Virginians, and it was a success.

The creative urges which had made Berkeley a playwright are precisely what sent him to Virginia to recoup his fortunes. He was tired of the role of cavalier in England, for he had played it to the hilt in the foppish court of Charles I and it did not entirely satisfy him. Virginia offered what he needed, a chance to expand the role of cavalier into that of creator and virtual king. By sheer force of vision he would create a commonwealth around himself, with all the settings of a prosperous society. There would be tobacco farms, of course, but also silk culture, fields of flax and hemp, and all the trappings of a pastoral agriculture. There would be cities, too, and shipyards. Amidst these scenes a contented populace would go about its tasks, confident in a governor of unimpeachable credentials, secure in Berkeley's ability to tame the Indian and to hold off English merchants seeking a monopoly of Virginia's trade. Such was the original vision. The most touching part is that the whole enterprise was to be a gift for the Stuart monarchs whom Berkeley loved so well. The ceremonies of le-

gitimacy always held his reverence, and having created around his own legitimacy a new jewel in England's crown, he would turn and offer it ceremonious-
ly to that crown.

It was a gallant wish, well realized. Step by step
from his arrival in 1642 Sir William made the commonwealth he had promised himself. His first step
was to move power from the crown toward the people,
as a sign of trust, and to make the point that this was
a separate and in some senses an independent society
he was building. He promised the people that the Virginia Company would never again rule, and that the
king's instructions ensured them forever the right to
trial by jury, the right to petition, and frequent elections of the House of Burgesses. The House of Burgesses itself would now sit with the governor and royal council as a coequal member of a Grand Assembly
which would become the supreme court of the land.
An act of 1643 further provided that the governor and
council "shall not lay any taxes or impositions on this
colony, their lands or commodities, otherwise than by
the authority of the Grand Assembly." Such taxes
were to be "levied and employed [strictly] as by the
Assembly shall be appointed." There would be no
taxation without representation.

Berkeley likewise encouraged the formation of new
counties, thereby offering local planters more oppor-
tunities to be appointed as justices and bringing the
law into newly settled areas. Control over religious

affairs was placed in the hands of vestrymen elected in each parish. The powers of government were spread widely.

The next step was to win successful planters to the governor's side. He did this by creating them justices, by listening to their opinions as expressed in the House of Burgesses, and by joining them in expeditions against the Indians. Berkeley also defended their interests against an England always seeking to extort every penny from the tobacco trade and from the sale of crown lands in Virginia. Made with extraordinary cavalier flair, these gestures established Berkeley's legitimacy with the planters. The problem then became to establish the planters' legitimacy with the rest of society.

It was no easy matter to take these "captains" and convince the public that they were gentlemen. Berkeley did it by sheer force of example, addressing them as "gentlemen" on a thousand ceremonious occasions until these crude planters became the objects of respect and of obedience. When they sat in the House of Burgesses, they received from Berkeley the elaborate veneration shown by the king toward the scions of ancient families sitting in the House of Commons. When they rode with him against the Indians, they cantered as courtiers at the side of a monarch, in panoply upon white horses to receive the homage of a subject race.

It was a brilliant act of creativity. It worked. By the end of the decade Berkeley was so popular and the

A Perfe&t Defcription of

# VIRGINIA:

*BEING*,

## A full and true Relation of the prefent State

of the Plantation , their Health, Peace, and Plenty: the number
of people, with their abundance of Cattell, Fowl, Fifh, &c. with feverall
forts of rich and good Commodities, which may there be had, either
Naturally, or by Art and Labour. Which we are fain to
procure from *Spain, France, Denmark, Swedeland, Germany,*
*Poland*, yea, from the *Eaft-Indies*. There
having been nothing related of the
true eftate of this Plantation thefe 25 years.

*Being fent from* Virginia , *at the requeft of a Gentleman of worthy note,*
*who defired to know the true State of* Virginia *as it now ftands.*

### ALSO,

## A Narration of the Countrey, within a few

dayes journey of *Virginia, Weft and by South,* where people come
to trade : being related to the Governour , Sir *William Berckley,*
who is to go himfelfe to difcover it with 30 horfe, and 50 foot,
and other things needfull for his enterprize.

*With the manner how the Emperor* Nichotawance

came to Sir *William Berckley* , attended with five petty Kings,
to doe Homage, and bring Tribute to King CHARLES. With his
folemne Proteftation , that the Sun and Moon fhould lofe
their Lights, before he (or his people in that Country)
fhould prove difloyall, but ever to keepe Faith
and Allegiance to King CHARLES.

*London*, Prind for *Richard Wodenoth*, at the Star under *Peters*
Church in *Cornhill*. 1649.

society so peaceful that Virginians had to be forced to set him aside for a parliamentary governor sent out with a fleet of Puritan rebels. Even before Charles II was restored to the English throne in 1660, Sir William Berkeley had been restored to the rule of his loyal society in Virginia. "My little government," he called it, as he set out to complete the unfinished lineaments of his plan.

On a visit to England, he pleaded with the king for more leeway in establishing a sound economy in the colony. "We cannot but resent," he complained, "that [under the proposed Acts of Trade and Navigation, restricting colonists to English shipping and markets] forty thousand Virginians should be impoverished to enrich little more than forty [London] merchants, who being the only legal buyers of our tobacco, give us what they please for it." He urged the king instead to allow Virginians to trade freely and to encourage them to develop other crops and infant industries. With assurances of the king's personal support, albeit with no cancellation of the first of these Navigation Acts, which was approved while he was in England, Berkeley returned to Virginia and committed his entire personal fortune to the creation of that diverse society he had long envisioned. He put money into silk manufacturing, encouraged the cultivation of flax and hemp, and sought to establish an urban center for trade which would entice the planters off their waterside plantations. He and his supporters also taxed the people to support these projects, but lightly and with due consent of the burgesses.

"My Virginia," Berkeley often said, but equally often it was "we." In the course of the years he had come to identify with Virginians. His actions were no longer part of a drama, but of an intense and abiding reality. It was with great happiness that he spoke of "the honor of so noble a work," and of "fair beginnings" carried on with "a joyful forwardness." The highlight of his life came when Virginia sent 100,000 pounds of silk to England and the king wore state garments woven of Virginia silk. In 1665 Berkeley wrote to an old friend, "I have received a letter from Harry Norwood in Tangier, who is now returned to England and hopes not to leave England any more, especially [to go to] either a garrison or to [a] plantation. For there is a great difference between these and Whitehall [i.e., England] in every cavalier's conception but mine, who am very well contented with my lot here."

But tobacco prices softened considerably toward the end of Berkeley's reign, and every dip in prices sent the populace into panics of uncertainty. Grumbling arose over paying even light taxes toward the maintenance of Berkeley's favorite projects. Some said that the money went instead into his favorites' pockets. Yet while Berkeley plowed his fortune into Virginia and himself into debt, his wealthy planter

friends held their fortunes aloof. At this moment
Berkeley's reputation became tarnished when he was
unable to keep the bankrupt Charles II from granting
the rich Northern Neck to a number of courtiers in
return for certain valuable considerations. By the
early 1670s the king was proposing to sell the whole
of Virginia to Lords Arlington and Culpeper. Thirty
years of careful tending of this loyal infant society
were to be dismissed in the wave of a scented glove.

Beset to rescue Virginia from tobacco prices and
from the king, Berkeley could not even defend the
colony against the more tangible threat of the Dutch
fleet which raided in 1673. Behind him lay a frantic
rabble he could not trust, before him the Dutch, and
across the Atlantic waited a king eager to put the colony in more profitable hands. After the partial success
of the Dutch, the fears and ambitions of Virginians
emerged against Sir William Berkeley. They awaited
only an occasion to seize power.

The catalyst was Nathaniel Bacon, a gentleman
also of unimpeachable English origins, who tore aside
the scrim on which Berkeley had painted his ideal
Virginia. In response to an Indian attack in 1676,
Bacon gathered freemen and planters into an army
and set out to annihilate all red men. His true aim was
to distinguish himself and to attack the governor. The
initial targets were Berkeley's "coddling" of the Indians, presumably in order to preserve their trade for
himself and his friends, and the "misuse" by the same

78

friends of tax revenues which might otherwise have strengthened defenses. But Bacon used the Indian issue to focus every fear of Virginians into a vortex of criticism against Berkeley. It was a fearful crime, they said, that men living on unreliable incomes in uncertain times should pay taxes to a regime of social tinkerers who had used their political powers to perpetuate their own control and to enrich themselves. Death at the hands of Indians was merely the final straw in a chain of abuses which demanded a change of regime.

Bacon and his followers succeeded in tearing the screen of legitimacy away from the Berkeley regime. Berkeley himself had settlers' blood on his hands, they pointed out, and the men around him had never been in any sense legitimate. Bacon subsequently delivered the final blow in an impassioned plea for his cause: "Let us trace these men in authority and favor to those hands the dispensation of the country's wealth has been committed; let us observe the sudden rise of their estates compared with the quality in which they first entered this country; or the reputation they have held here amongst wise and discerning men. And let us see whether their extractions and education have not been vile, and by what pretense of learning and virtue they could [come] so soon into employments of so great trust and consequence. Let us also consider whether any public work for our safety and defence or for the advancement and propagation of trade, liberal arts or sciences is here extant in any [way] adequate to our vast charge. Now let us compare these things together and see what sponges have sucked up the public treasure and whether it has not been privately contrived away by unworthy favorites and juggling parasites whose tottering fortunes have been repaired and supported at the public charge. Now if it be so, judge what greater guilt can [there] be than to offer to pry into these and to unriddle the mysterious wiles of a powerful cabal."

Once the emperor's nakedness was seen, however, it was not easy to build a substitute legitimacy out of the inchoate fears and unmet ambitions which had coalesced into rebellion. Bacon offered himself as the new cavalier, and offered "gentle" status to the planters who followed him, in unconscious imitation of Berkeley. Berkeley fought back in his old style, accusing Bacon of discarding "gentlemen" of "eminent services." Bacon himself, he observed, was given to "atheistical swearing" and had about him "none but the lowest of the people," a "rabble." But once the issue was raised, neither side could have had enough phrases to inflate itself into an acceptable imitation of gentility. Virginia dissolved into the eternal confusion of a society in which legitimacy was all too obviously an artificial construct. Bacon died, Berkeley was recalled to England, and a new governor was sent out.

For Berkeley, the scenery had fallen down, leaving an old man who had once wanted to make a gift for his sovereign. He wrote to England, "I am so over-weaned with riding into all parts of this country to stop this violent rebellion that I am not able to support myself at this age six months longer and therefore on my knees I beg his sacred majesty would send a more vigorous governor." His epitaph was uttered by the council: "He left no part of a prudent governor or valiant general unperformed." In Virginia, this was not enough. Legitimacy had to grow from within.

∾

Time would repair what man had marred. Over the fifty years that followed Bacon's rebellion the sources of disorder eased into a sort of social truce, the bases of the society shifted slowly toward social order, and legitimacy itself arrived in the form of an aristocracy of accepted social authority. The result in Virginia was a genuine and stable social order characteristic of the colonial South. A source of pride to many, its fragilities continued to reveal that in America it was not always easy to escape from nature into the refuge of the state.

No document relates these changes, so they must remain forever a source of speculation. The initial event seems to have been the removal of certain irritations and the regularization of others. The narrative of 1673 had placed particular stress on the number of single men willing to share the plunder with a successful invader. With time, male predominance gave way to an even balance of men and women.

Family life became the overwhelming norm. Despite a mortality which surpassed that of New England and sometimes that of Europe, men and women shaped their emotional commitments around one another and their children. When death struck, kin and friends eased the survivor into another marriage or cared for the orphans. The lives of most men came to revolve around such ordinary commitments.

Ambitions, possibly, were readjusted to a familial scale as a rivalry of freebooters gave way to a simpler desire for a sufficiency. In spite of large plantations, the resources of land and of kin and friendship connections were usually enough to guarantee subsistence for a family. Here and there in the interstices of the plantation system a small man could do better than subsistence.

By the second quarter of the eighteenth century, too, persons who had been raised in England became more rare, and so did the mockery aimed at men who claimed social superiority. The largest proportion of Virginians had been raised in the colony, and the "captains" and "justices" of the local scene were the only social betters most of them had experienced. In this limited way such men gained acceptance.

As for forces outside the colony, the vagaries of the staple crop economy and of the British Empire became a known climate of enterprise. In 1660 the imposition of the first royal Navigation Act requiring tobacco to be shipped in English ships to England had evoked a bitter resentment. But by 1725 Navigation Acts were a fact of life, and the navy they helped support had more than once seen the crop safely across a hostile Atlantic. By 1725 the Dutch, who had formerly offered the best terms of trade for tobacco, could no longer offer this guarantee. More, London rather than Amsterdam was now the credit center of the European world. Although contractions there occasionally led to a painful shrinking of credit in the colonies, in most years London offered easy terms to planters caught up in the insatiable need to buy more land and more labor in order to produce more tobacco and so maintain income in times of falling prices. Loans or advances on crops also helped tide over the impecunious planter, enabling him to maintain his life-style. It was a fragile but familiar system to colonial Virginians.

Within this system royal authority became more consistent and also more light-handed. England had determined that the colonial rebellions of the seventeenth century would not be repeated and that the Navigation Acts would be enforced. By the 1730s Virginia and North and South Carolina were all under royal governors. Maryland, while restored to the newly anglicized lords of Baltimore, was kept under the royal eye. Royal judges and customs collectors had become established facts of life, as was the royal authority behind the justices in most counties. At the same time both England and her governors had learned the lessons of the previous century. Sudden shifts in policy, or a governor who collected too small a coterie of local supporters, or who interfered with representatives, justices, or vestrymen, could have violent consequences. By and large the governor was left to reach his own accommodation with the aspiring men of his colony, with the understanding that a careless governor could lose if it came to a formal appeal of his authority back to England.

Slavery might be seen as incidental to this gradual disappearance or regularization of the instabilities – the sex ratio, expectations, social perspective, the economy, and the empire – which had forced Berkeley from office. Indisputably the rapid development of slavery arose simply from an economic demand for labor which could not be met efficiently or at all by large-scale importation of white servants from Britain. But the fact is that slavery had implications for the social synthesis which emerged in the eighteenth-century South, and for the role of the emergent aristocracy which was the accepted leader of that synthesis.

For that aristocracy was built above all upon slavery, and slavery had certain indisputable advantages. In the place of the constant influx of white servants came instead a flood of black slaves. The supply of white servants was uncertain and depended in part upon the treatment of this rambunctious lot in the colonies as reported back to England. Rambunctious

84

or not, servants became free, which meant a constant injection of new, foreign, and poor men into the body politic. Slaves were brought in regardless of conditions in numbers which depended solely on the enterprise of the slavers and on the planters' purses. Slaves were servants for life, and by the eighteenth century, so were their descendants. Slaves had to accept the legitimacy of their masters and of the state on plain penalty of death. In short, in slaves the planter South found not only a secure labor supply but also a captive audience for its evolving sense of its own legitimacy.

In some sense slaves became the captive audience for poor whites and planters alike, and against this background were played out the ceremonies of an increasing mutual acceptance between yeoman and planter in colonial Virginia. In another sense slaves became the cornerstone of a society in which even white liberties were tempered. The suffrage had already been allowed to narrow somewhat, and despite the reduction in the influx of white servants and eventual freemen, the right to vote never again expanded to its previous breadth. Economic power was already focusing progressively in the hands of the few, until in some areas in the eighteenth century the richest tenth of men owned between half and two-thirds of the total wealth of the society. Slavery only accelerated this concentration of political and economic power by reducing a rapidly growing and problematic white constituency and by focusing immense, self-reproducing economic power in the hands of a few. Furthermore, slaves were the prototype for the deference which native whites were expected to show their betters. Slavery permitted the attendance of liveried house slaves whose gaze, focused upon the ceremonious comings and goings of the master, gave a cue which others might imitate. If the liberties of the eighteenth-century South were somewhat fewer than those of Pennsylvania or of New England, slavery may explain why.

Be that as it may, such an aristocracy did evolve upon the pedestals of tobacco and of slavery and it was accepted. Fifty years before, in the time of Nathaniel Bacon, it would have been absurd to identify an "aristocracy." Bacon had mocked Berkeley's "gentlemen" but could not produce his own. As late as 1725 such pretensions were equally hilarious in the Carolinas. Yet already in the later seventeenth century Virginia planters had numbered among themselves a few score sons of acknowledged gentle English families. By the first half of the eighteenth century their sons and daughters had intermarried with each other and with the children of less distinguished but equally wealthy planters, and their children in turn had grown into a third generation of wealth and position. Suddenly names meant something, especially to a native populace to whom Byrd, Carter,

86

and Beverly were all the distinction they had ever known.

Robert Beverly is a splendid example. His father, Robert Beverly, could at least claim gentle Yorkshire ancestry and had money with him on arriving in 1663. "The Major," as he was known, became a large planter and a royal councillor who stood by Sir William Berkeley throughout Bacon's Rebellion. Major Beverly was a loud, rough man who burned the fields of planters who would not limit production, cursed every subsequent royal governor as a tyrant, and nearly ended his days in jail. But his was an adequate foundation for a son educated in England and born to his father's wealth. The son Robert Beverly retained many of the crudities of the Major, including a tendency to ridicule all royal authority as despotic and illegitimate, but he was indisputably a gentleman. His sons in turn, as they clove to the expanding intricacies of the tobacco connection with England, and of slavery, would be more truly gentle.

In such men time produced not only order but legitimacy in the colonial South. And the legitimacy of an indigenous aristocracy three generations in the making in turn served as the basis of an accepted social order. Robert Beverly symbolized this aristocracy, and in his *History of Virginia* he was the witness of its success. As early as 1705 Beverly could describe the civil polity of Virginia with a confidence previously impossible. His chapter titles bespeak an inordinate calm: "Of the Constitution of Government in Virginia; Of the Courts of Law in Virginia; Of the Militia in Virginia; and Of Servants and Slaves in Virginia."

"Of the Courts of Law in Virginia" speaks dispassionately of everyday details of jurisdictions and of officers, then moves on to consider juries: "The way of impaneling juries to serve in this [higher] court is thus: The sheriff and his deputies every morning the court sits goes about town summoning the best of gentlemen who resort thither from all parts of the country. By this means are procured the best juries this country can afford, for [no] particular county [can] afford so many qualified persons as are to be found because of the great resort of gentlemen from all parts of the colony as well to see fashions as to discharge their business. Nor is [it] necessary there to distinguish the several customs of particular places, the whole country being as one neighborhood and having the same tenures of land usages and customs."

Beverly continued to the effect that "in criminal matters this method is a little altered, because a knowledge of the life and conversation of the party may give light to the jury in their verdict. For this reason a writ summons six of the nearest neighbors to the criminal, who must be of the same county wherein he lived. [The panel of twelve is then] filled up with the names of other gentlemen in the town to be of the jury for the trial of that criminal. If the prisoner have a mind to challenge the jurors, the same liberty is allowed him there as in England, and if the panel fall short it must be made up of the bystanders." The county courts handled lesser cases in the same manner, their chief concerns being hog thieves and orphans.

Servants and slaves in Virginia, according to Beverly's essay, offered no urgent problems to the local justices. "The work of servants and slaves is no other than what every common freeman does. All servants have their complaints heard without fee, [and] servants' complaints are to be received at any time in court and shall not be delayed for want of form but the merits of the complaint must be immediately enquired into by the justices. If a master shall at any time disobey an order of court made upon any complaint of a servant, the court is empowered to remove such servant forthwith to another master who will be kinder. No master of a servant can make a new bargain for service or other matter with his servant without the privity and consent of a justice of the peace. For no people abhor the thought of ill-usage more than the Virginians."

It was finally a social order which Beverly depicted. His *History* was the landmark of an age in which gentlemen mingled with bystanders on terms of accepted social and political leadership. All lived within the "one neighborhood" so comfortably described by

Beverly. Every line spoke of that legitimacy which Ratcliffe had parodied and which Berkeley could only counterfeit. Soon Maryland and South Carolina would follow suit.

Virginians fled willingly to the social order led by their gentry. They were by and large comfortable within its deferential relationships. They never asked whether its liberties were greater or fewer than they might otherwise have had, as an accepted and reciprocal social relationship was too valuable to destroy. Gentlemen could be gentle, and lead, so long as bystanders could vote or were considered. It was a haven after a century of trouble.

There remained an air of artifice about the Virginia gentlemen of the eighteenth century. In Virginia the perfunctory ceremonial relations of councillors and governor were replaced by an elaborate courtesy. When the burgesses joined in, the bowing and scrapings, polite addresses, and gallant replies exceeded Sir William Berkeley's visions. The content of these exchanges sometimes expressed opposition but this was hidden in an ornate language by which, as if by mutual agreement, all parties publicly embellished one another's reputations. Early in the century the drama moved to a larger stage in Williamsburg, where witnesses could not fail to be impressed by the elaborate play of mutual respect. In this way locals and governors verified one another's legitimacy. They must have understood that it was a necessary game which they played so unceasingly.

The English education valued by the transitional generation of planters was an essential part of these trappings. Sir William had played his part naturally in the ceremonies of legitimacy, but his assistants had been clumsy. The next generation of sons went to England to learn how to do it right. They returned laundered of dirt, dressed in lace, and sporting the proper legalisms. Such men could serve as acolytes in the ceremonies presided over by a royal governor without the fear that they might miss a cue. Some eventually outperformed the governors. They did equally well in county courts, where the mockery died away.

The emergent aristocrats also threw themselves, a little too wildly, into further ceremonies which established their social authority. In gambling and in horse racing the young bloods could show that they were bold enough to lead in time of war and careless enough of wealth to be trusted by all. In treating the local militia to punch they offered a means by which the populace could respond, namely with a hearty cheer for the squire who provided the refreshments. The planters likewise appeared as mediators, doctors, and even priests in a score of lesser exchanges which verified their status and in which the people played out their recognition.

The result was a certain brittleness, or a sense of men isolated amidst their own performances. Not in an uncomfortable isolation, but indeed in a gracious one, in which the voters confirmed their betters at every election. But isolation all the same. William Byrd, master of Westover, former burgess and king's councillor, provides an example. His diary for 1709 begins: "I rose at 5 o'clock this morning and read a chapter in Hebrew and 200 verses in Homer's *Odyssey*. I ate milk for breakfast. I said my prayers. Jenny and Eugene were whipped. I danced my dance. I read law in the morning and Italian in the afternoon . . ." Daily, Byrd said his prayers, "danced his dance" for exercise right after breakfast, spoke to his overseers or to his wife about disobedient house slaves, perhaps saw the local parson or a client seeking a favor, read in two languages, gave his wife "a flourish," and went to bed. Twice a year he rode to Williamsburg to join in the minuet of colonial government. Always the impression is of a man doing precisely what was expected of him. There was no joy or spontaneity about this cavalier. Michael Wigglesworth, trapped in his own conscience, was no more pitiful than Councillor William Byrd of Virginia. Moreover, Byrd and his like clung to their ceremonies long after there was no danger of another Nathaniel Bacon.

Why? In one sense the drama of social and political legitimacy laid out in eighteenth-century Virginia was no more than the history of the evolving state in

*William Byrd, from a painting by an unknown artist (London 1692–95?), courtesy of Colonial Williamsburg Incorporated.*

the modern era, a state never entirely secure. In another sense, it reflected the peculiar sensitivities of English culture. Fear of the impending death of their culture has ever spurred Englishmen to master the ceremonies of social legitimacy. It has made "English gentleman" a byword for snobs the world around. In the New World this sensitivity turned to near hysteria: John Rolfe had to ask official permission to marry Pocohontas, and had to reassure his countrymen that he was not "going native" out of sheer sexual desire but would convert the maiden. English, Christian culture must triumph over pagan dissolution. Possibly it was only this recurrent fear which kept the Virginia gentlemen so assiduously dancing their dances.

If it was English culture they wished to preserve, they succeeded too well, for the model was too compelling. One thinks of William Fitzhugh, of Stafford County, Virginia, who in 1686 offered to trade his entire plantations, valued at £600 per annum, for "an estate of inheritance in land there [in England] of two or three hundred pounds a year, or in houses in any town of three or four hundred pounds a year." Or one pictures William Byrd, a generation later, back from London in body but in spirit hanging on every bit of news from the mother country. Out on their plantations alone, or when they talked, so largely to one another, these men knew where the only true society for a gentleman lay. Their ceremonies were in part a longing for another place, another time.

93

Regardless of these concerns, the insistence on an aristocratic model of society was also an attempt to cover up the vulnerability of all legitimacies in the New World. Everywhere in early America some model of society had to be constantly reasserted in the face of realities which eroded all legitimacy. In Virginia these realities were unusually troublesome. Only in juxtaposition to a wise aristocracy could slavery be justified and fear eased. Only under the leadership of a calm aristocracy could a turbulent majority possessed of the suffrage be channeled into its due and deferential course. Only a spendthrift aristocracy could cover the insecurities of the tobacco economy with a gloss of insouciance, and so maintain control. Things had not changed so much since Governor Berkeley's day, as William Byrd discovered. Arching over all was the terrible nakedness of all legitimacies in colonial America. The insistence on legitimacy runs like a central thread through all the social efforts of leaders from New England to the later colonial society of Georgia. Particularly in the South, the recentness with which disorder had given way to legitimacy and the transparency of the devices used to reach it made the planter synthesis especially vulnerable. It is a measure of these same social vulnerabilities that so many men subscribed to that synthesis.

◦～◦

Outside the world of the gentry lay still another world. This was what the earliest South would have become had there been no tobacco, or rice, and had no gentry arisen around these. William Byrd visited it while supervising the running of the dividing line between Virginia and North Carolina, though as much of this society fell within Virginia as within North Carolina. In his Addisonian "History of the Dividing Line," Byrd referred to this other society as "lubberland": "Both cattle and hogs ramble in the neighboring marshes and swamps, where they maintain themselves the whole winter long, and are not fetched home till the spring. Thus these indolent wretches, during one half of the year, lose the advantage of the milk of their cattle, as well as their dung, and many of the poor creatures perish in the more by this ill management. Some who pride themselves more upon industry than their neighbors, will, now and then, in compliment to their cattle, cut down a tree whose limbs are laden with moss. The trouble would be too great to climb the tree in order to gather this provender, so the shortest way (which in this country is always counted the best) is to fell it, just like the lazy Indians.

The only business here is the raising of hogs, which is managed with the least trouble, and affords the diet they are most fond of. The truth of it is, these inhabitants of North Carolina devour so much swine's flesh that it fills them full of gross humors. [This results in] yaws, [which] first seizes the throat, next the palate, and lastly shows its spite on the poor nose of which

95

'tis apt in a small time treacherously to undermine the foundation. Surely there is no place in the world where the inhabitants live with less labor than in North Carolina. It approaches nearer the description of lubberland than any other, by the great felicity of the climate, the easiness of raising provisions, and the slothfulness of the people.

I believe this [Edenton, N.C.] is the only metropolis in the Christian or Mahometan world where there is neither church, chapel, mosque, synagogue or any other place of public worship of any sect or religion whatsoever. They account it among their greatest advantages that they are not priestridden, not remembering that the clergy is rarely guilty of bestriding such as have the misfortune to be poor. One thing [which] may be said for the inhabitants of this province, [is] that they are not troubled by any religious fumes. What little devotion they may happen to have is much more private than their vices.

A citizen here is accounted extravagant if he has ambition enough to aspire to a brick chimney. Justice herself is but indifferently lodged, the court house having the air of a common tobacco house. They are rarely guilty of flattering or making court to their governors, but treat them with all excesses of freedom and familiarity. They are of the opinion that their rulers would be apt to grow insolent if they grew rich, and for this reason take care to keep them poorer and more dependent, if possible, than the saints in New

England used to do their governors. Another reason the government there is so loose and the laws so feebly executed is that every one does just what seems good in his own eyes. If the governor's hands have been weak in that province, much weaker then were the hands of the magistrate, who though he might have had the virtue to endeavor to punish offenders, which very rarely happened, [found himself] quite impotent for want of ability to put it into execution. One bold magistrate, taking upon him to order a fellow to the stocks for being disorderly in his drink was, for his intemperate zeal, carried thither himself and narrowly escaped being whipped by the rabble into the bargain."

There was concern beneath Byrd's sarcasm, as if the sheer laziness of this world would dissolve all the careful civilizings of his class. He tried to control it with the witty prose fashionable in England, but returned obsessively to the fearful "laziness" of lubberland.

"Lubberland" was an extreme version of a rural subsistence society found widely in the newer and in the western parts of the rural South. And lubberland, in this larger sense, had values of its own other than those ridiculed by Byrd. Devereux Jarratt, growing up in rural Virginia in the 1740s, described it this way: "None of my ancestors on either side were rich or great, but had the character of honesty and industry, by which they lived in good repute among their

97

neighbors, free from real want and above the frowns of the world. [We] always had plenty of plain food and raiment, wholesome and good. Our food was altogether the produce of the farm, or plantation, except a little sugar, and our raiment was altogether my mother's manufacture, except our hats and shoes, the latter of which we never put on but in the winter season. We made no use of tea or coffee for breakfast, or at any other time, nor did I know a single family that made any use of them. We were accustomed to look upon what were called *gentle folks* as beings of a superior order. For my part I was quite shy of them. A periwig, in those days, was a distinguishing badge of gentle folk; and when I saw a man riding the road, near our house, with a wig on, it would so alarm my fears and give me such a disagreeable feeling that, I daresay, I would run off as for my life. Such ideas of the difference between *gentle* and *simple* were, I believe, universal among all my rank and age."

Jarratt confirmed Byrd's fears of lubberland. He lived in an area by no means as isolated as the North Carolina–Virginia border, yet as a child he had so little daily contact with "gentle folk" that he would run away in amazed fear on those occasions when he saw a gentleman. His family was equally unacquainted with their "betters" and evidently had no need of them. They were economically self-sufficient, morally self-guided, and utterly removed from the machinations of higher colonial or imperial politics. As in lubberland, there was no necessity for a William Byrd.

By the time Jarrett grew up, a new religion was giving confidence to his world. He had explained his religious upbringing in the rudimental terms which might have been expected: "My parents neither sought nor expected any titles, honors, or great things for their children. Their highest ambition was to teach their children to read, write, and understand the fundamental rules of arithmetic. They also taught us short prayers and made us very perfect in repeating the *Church Catechism*." After a long history of this simple social and religious background, Jarrett's backcountry encountered the revived religion of the Methodist, Presbyterian, and Baptist missionaries who penetrated even to the Appalachians by 1760. The new religion was a galvanizing experience for men attached to the simplicities in which they had been raised, for they found a religion which made simple folk into the inheritors of the earth. The God of such "new lights" as the Baptists intended men to seek their own earnest ways and to live plainly, without presumption. Armed with this knowledge the simple folk of the backcountry would turn with scorn to the riders of horses, the wearers of periwigs, and the leaders of men. Byrd had had cause to be apprehensive.

The Baptist revival in Virginia took a course similar to that of the Great Awakening in New England. But it had a special edge of social criticism. Revived preachers alarmed individual souls, whose fears led them to God. These reborn individuals gathered into tightly knit communities described in their records as "we," as "our society," or as "brethren." The moral authority of these communities was absolute over every individual and over the preachers they installed. Equality and simplicity in all things became the order of the day. Simple in their speech, in their dress, and in their language, members of reborn communities frowned where gentlemen smiled, walked where gentry rode, and avoided with deliberate passion the cockfights, militia-day punchbowls, and taverns where gentle young bloods displayed their social leadership. The gentry did not miss the message of these somber souls on the outside of their public ceremonies.

The Baptists and their like had opted out of the hierarchical social system led by gentlemen. Their very behavior labeled their superiors as corrupt. Virginia gentlemen understood that this withdrawal was a threat to a moral leadership which they had exercised as much from horseback as from the front pews of Anglican churches. They saw that this rejection of their moral authority reflected in turn on the authority of the colonial government which they had so nearly legitimized and which in turn had helped legitimize them. It was no consolation that so far it was only the religious authority of the Anglican church, the county courts, the House of Burgesses, and the royal council and governor which were challenged by Baptist communities demanding licensing of their preachers and an end to religious censorship of their message. A demand for religious authority in the hands of leveling congregations had clear political implications in the rejection of all hierarchies of authority including the civil.

The gentry therefore perceived that the revival was a "mutiny against the authority of the land." Privately with whips and publicly with repressive legislation the gentlemen hierarchs of the royal colony of Virginia sought to put down a mutiny which in their terms could only end in a chaos reminiscent of earliest Virginia. They failed. Baptist pressure rose to meet gentry repression. The cultural war between Baptists and gentry was papered over in the early stages of the American Revolution, in the 1760s and early 1770s, as both sides rejected Parliament's right to tax Americans. But when after independence the time came to write a state constitution and to conduct state politics, it became clear once again that in the religious realm, as by ever more explicit implication in the political, there were mutually futile conceptions of a legitimate social order struggling against each other in Virginia. The political issues were more subtle here than in Massachusetts; in Virginia the prime source of concern for the gentry was that in an increasing number of constituencies they were having a hard time getting elected. The voters preferred ordinary men like themselves, who could be subordinated to local wishes. This was a logical extension into politics of Baptist principles concerning the ministry, and again it eroded the hierarchical world of the gentry. By the 1780s some Virginia gentlemen, among them George Washington, had begun to despair over the future of a hierarchical order in Virginia. They were ready to welcome the new federal Constitution as a guarantee that somewhere a centralized state led by substantial men would rule. They had reached the same conclusions as their counterparts in Massachusetts.

৫৵৹

Late seventeenth-century New England had manifested a cultural opposition similar to that of the mid-eighteenth-century South. The villagers of Salem had used the legitimacy of an intense religious orthodoxy to carry out a campaign against periwigs and against all the worldly presumptions pressing down upon them. The folk of the Southern backcountry later joined a similar campaign directed from the pulpit. Whatever the differences between Northern and Southern localism – the Northern had a history in England that the Southern did not; the Northern was on occasion more explicitly political than the Southern – there was an inner similarity which stemmed from a common American experience. Isolation, simplicity, and self-sufficiency had been a way of life for much of the population in both regions.

In both cases men were asking to be left alone in their relative equality, with the means to be modestly self-supporting and the right to shape their own moral worlds. This required local control of local religious and political leaders. It meant that a religious and political leadership based on a cosmopolitan gentry elite operating and gaining further power and legitimacy from a hierarchy of governmental institutions culminating in a central nation-state had to be rejected as immoral. The suppression of political discourse before the Revolution, the religious awakening of the mid-eighteenth century, and the moralistic overtones of localism explain why the initial form of explicit localism was so often evangelistic. This evangelical localism was nonetheless increasingly political in its demands. Yet in Virginia as in New England, localism failed to articulate itself as a full-fledged political ideology. It was everywhere redolent of a disgraced sectarianism and at the same time it was too unprecedented. Nor, in Virginia any more than in New England, were localism's proponents yet ready to accept the individualism implicit in their own emphasis on the ordinary man and on his freedom from higher authorities. Individualism was still a bastard child.

Such men as Byrd and the Mathers can also be compared. All stood for a principle of legitimacy which was hierarchical; all trusted to the ceremonies by which the superior reinforced their social position; all placed in the hands of this elite the essential powers of a hierarchy of institutions reaching up to the crown. Their successors during the Revolution replaced the crown with powerful state governments and with a federal nation-state. With all its variations their world was familiar to European intellectuals of the time. Weighty volumes ornamented the layered world of these hierarchs. It was impossible to argue against them in open debate. Yet they were never securely founded in the realities of the American environment and so could nowhere gain that overwhelming acceptance which was the prerequisite of legitimacy. In the New World, their legitimacy was too painfully artificial in its creation. If localism was an environment without an ideology, in America hierarchy was an ideology without a secure environment. This is what the gentlemen of Virginia and of New England discovered during the American Revolution.

The principles struggling so vainly in the American land were the same principles facing human beings in Europe, only here they were shaped by circumstance into a recurring deadlock. If everywhere in the Western world the simple universals first pursued behind the plow grounded all such debates in an eternal reluctance to change, it was also true that everywhere an embryonic individualism pulled at the restraints of localism and of aristocracy alike, threatening a new age of Western society. This drama, too, was to be more dramatic in America, as would become clear by the end of the Revolution.

# Conclusion

## The problem of political legitimacy in early America

ALL legitimacies were vulnerable in early America. Too artificial, too obvious, or too untried, every principle of social and political authority was eroded either by the colonists' skepticism or by other principles also striving for acceptance. In such an environment it was not only the early Carolina proprietors' famous scheme for an ornate artificial nobility which went under; in a sense every pretense to a legitimate social order was threatened by the same conditions.

Most prominent among these pretenses were a hierarchical principle of authority familiar to Britons, and a pious localism more prevalent in America than elsewhere in Western society. In the former God parceled down his authority through kings, officials, and aristocrats. The people's share was often passed upward again through restricted elections and came downward to them once more in the form of authority. In the latter, God conveyed his authority directly to the self-sufficient community of believers and little more was required. Neither principle could establish itself as the legitimate principle of political authority in early America.

John Winthrop had striven to create a degree of hierarchical power, as can be seen in his stern lecture on liberty. For a time he succeeded, but in the end he failed. His periwigged successors dared not lecture as sternly nor were they backed by such pressure of circumstance. When England called on Massachusetts to assume its place in the ladder of the state these men responded as they had to respond and took their places under a royal governor. Salem impeached them as surely as John Winthrop had ever been impeached. The villagers failed, but their implicit indictment of evolving social and political hierarchies lived on in the New England consciousness. A localism in which God spoke directly to each village and to each congregation, confirming the rightness of their ways and reaffirming their authority against all outsiders, had been reborn on American soil. It would be revived yet again in the Great Awakening, both in New England and in Virginia, and it would not surrender its rebirth in the name of any alternatives. Yet, although an evangelical localism described admirably the conditions of American life, it was also vulnerable. It was at once too old to be fashionable and too untried as a dominant principle to be taken seriously by educated men even in Massachusetts.

Virginians had better success with a social and

political hierarchy which in the beginning faced only ridicule instead of a sanctified opposition reaching back into the villages of medieval England. In time the planters became gentlemen and the legal system which they so thoroughly mastered became the accepted matrix of a legitimate social order. Yet the conditions of American life could not be denied. By the middle of the eighteenth century history had recreated itself here in the form of an evangelical localism indigenous to Virginia and ever more critical of an even more nervous gentry. Neither side entirely recognized the legitimacy of the other, and their weapons became superciliousness and horsewhips on the one side and a caustic piety on the other.

By the time of the American Revolution these rival and unsuccessful legitimacies had become the prevailing characteristic of American culture. Even in the apparently peaceful middle colonies, the last decades of the eighteenth century revealed a fear that the inherent localism of the American experience would destroy all government. Pennsylvania is an example. Here, as in New York, the localism appeared at first glance to be the "localism" merely of a diverse population, each element of which was struggling for its share of resources. Even this was problem enough, as in Pennsylvania the Quakers, Germans, and Scotch-Irish, and in New York the Dutch, the English, and Long Islanders originally from New England, all fell out with one another. But beneath these apparent instances of a healthy, pluralistic politics of openly contending interests lay a localism more profound than the transient demands of ethnic interest.

In Pennsylvania, for example, the revivalist Presbyterianism of the Scotch-Irish was openly hostile to the authority of a church hierarchy dominated by a ministerial elite itself well educated, elegantly dressed, and Eastern. Their awakened Presbyterianism rejected such pretensions in favor of local control of ministers by a revived laity. Old Light Presbyterians labeled this "anarchy." Anarchy seemed closer when, in the 1760s, some of these same Scotch-Irish settlers, believing themselves inadequately protected against hostile Indians by the Quakers in the Pennsylvania assembly, took matters into their own hands by massacring every Indian within reach. At one point they marched on Philadelphia, threatening to bring down the government, and were stopped only by a fast-talking Benjamin Franklin. Their attitudes toward the colonial government were ambivalent. On the one hand they demanded protection and enhanced representation. On the other, as the American Revolution soon revealed, in their deepest thoughts they preferred to do without higher governments.

Benjamin Franklin left for England immediately after this incident, the Paxton Rebellion, to try to persuade the crown to take over the proprietary government of Pennsylvania. Partly, he did this out of personal ambition. He hoped to be made royal governor of Pennsylvania. But Franklin and his ally Joseph Galloway were also convinced that only the backing of the crown could legitimize the government and established politicians of Pennsylvania and hold that government together in the face of the searing contempt of local interests and of local rebellions. This explains the irony that placed Benjamin Franklin in London, pleading with the crown to take over control of Pennsylvania, at the moment that Parliament infuriated his American constituents with the Stamp Tax. He was trying to buttress a colonial hierarchy with a royal authority in the face of a corrosive American environment.

The eternal insecurity of both would-be legitimacies in early America may help explain one paradox of eighteenth-century American history. It has been observed that just when the gentlemen of colonial America were reaching political maturity, and were seeking a firmer political control of the economies and societies evolving beneath them, they also embraced the legitimacy of the British Empire. They fought with their English governors for political authority within each colony, yet they simultaneously laid down the angry petitions against the "slavery" of colonial status and the "burden" of the Navigation Acts, which had been characteristic of the late seventeenth century. They embraced the style, the role, and the obedience of loyal British subjects. One reason was that the de facto burden of imperial restrictions on colonial politics and trade grew lighter as "salutary neglect" of the colonies became the policy of a Britain occupied with European wars. Could it be that the empire won allegiance also, however, because an imperial hierarchy flowing from God through the king and out by way of the king in council to the royal governors in America did wonders for the legitimacy of colonial gentlemen? The polite Mathers needed help in governing Massachusetts over the voices of a multitude of skeptical sectarians out in the villages. Even the Virginians, vastly more able governors, seem to have found the trappings of royal government a nice addition to their regalia as they set out to win the locals' allegiance. Franklin perceived that he had no choice but to seek out the crown. The empire may have had its uses in an America where no legitimacy was secure and where a localistic alternative to hierarchical authority had everywhere begun to assert itself.

Could American gentlemen have overestimated their success when they later cast off the mantle of empire? They represented only one of two rival and not entirely successful legitimacies in colonial America. Was it wise of them to embark upon a revolution which would remove the king and expose them as sole masters of the social hierarchy at home? They were so sure of their acceptance in Americans' eyes that they never seem to have asked the question. Perhaps they imagined that their leadership in the resistance to British taxation would renew their legitimacy by showing the advantages of a native aristocracy. They were wrong. Rural Americans had never been as concerned about British taxation as were these colonial aristocrats, for it was the aristocrats whose legislative powers were eroded by the new device of direct taxation by Parliament and who were most alarmed. Rural Americans were more concerned about the power of all aristocracies, British or American. The Loyalists tried to warn their fellow American aristocrats that aristocratic rule in the colonies was too fragile to dispense with the symbol even of a mistaken king. They were branded "Tories" and sent into exile. But the Tories were right.

No sooner had the Revolution begun than voices arose everywhere in the colonies, saying "We have not cast off a British aristocracy to be saddled with an American one." These voices unburdened themselves in speeches and crude pamphlets from Maine to Pennsylvania and far into North Carolina. Any doubt as to whether localism was strong everywhere in America ended with the Revolution. In all colonies men asked for "no governair but the guvernor of the univarse"; they invoked the ancient Saxon constitutions of an imagined Germanic tribal past; they asked for state constitutions without governors, for legislatures without upper houses, and for lower houses made up of local representatives annually elected by universal male suffrage and severely restricted in their ability to tax or indeed to govern the people at all. In some cases they demanded that localities have the right to review whatever legislation emerged from such a hobbled government. In Pennsylvania, localists successfully wrote nearly all these demands into the state constitution of 1776. Worse still, localists elected persons who were not aristocrats to carry these opinions into practice under whatever sort of state constitutions they got. The leaders of the revolutionary movement reacted in shock. Washington, Adams, even Madison wrote letters to one another and to friends, asking what could be done with a people who would not always recognize the legitimacy of their natural or even of their elected leaders. The world view nurtured in the villages of New England and reborn in rural Virginia returned to haunt them as soon as these more prominent patriots had got rid of the British. The riposte of the aristocrats was a federal Constitution designed once and for all to ensure the election of "the better sort" to the offices of a powerful central state.

The corrosive legacy of a world in which no political principle was secure had come home even to revolutionary America. It raised in James Madison's mind the prospect of an ungovernable America. Yet out of the struggle between these vulnerable legitimacies, hierarchy and evangelical localism, emerged a political principle which transcended them both and which was to gain as much true legitimacy as any principle ever has had in America. Oddly, this principle arose in the mind of James Madison, otherwise an advocate of "the better sort" and a friend of the Constitution. Somehow, as he witnessed the fruitless partisan political struggles of the revolutionary era, Madison glimpsed momentarily a new society and a new politics. He described these in his *Federalist* essay number ten, and in this brief essay he portrayed the Constitution as the framework for a new principle of human society and of political order.

What was Madison's vision, half-glimpsed amid the clash of would-be legitimacies? It was a vision which would not have been unfamiliar to thoughtful Britons of the time, above all to Adam Smith. It involved first of all a rejection of previous principles of authority. Men in their localities, assembled as the popular majority, could not be trusted because of their tendency to abuse the rights of minorities. A government without structure would be easily captured by such a ruthless majority. A government without powers beyond the power of the majority would not have the strength to defend all its citizens from the occasionally erroneous will of that majority. Localism, in its latter-day garb of majority rule – pure popular sovereignty and nearly nonexistent government – was therefore an unacceptable basis for government. Madison then flirted wistfully with the virtues of wise leadership, but had to admit that "it is in vain to say that enlightened statesmen will be able to adjust clashing interests and render them all subservient to the public good. Enlightened statesmen will not always be at the helm." How then could men be governed?

Madison began with the sacredness of the individual. The right to the full expression of individual uniqueness was the basic value of Madison's new world. "The diversity in the faculties of men, from which the rights of property originate" could not be extinguished and must be allowed expression. "The protection of these faculties is the first object of government." More, the individual has a right to political expression, so individuals assembled in the form of the people, and inevitably the majority of these individuals, must elect the government. Power must flow from sovereign individuals to the state.

The problem with a society based on individual self-expression was first that this involved the acceptance of a teemingly diverse society in which individual interests, selfishly pursued, accumulated into interest groups struggling for power. Yet Madison perceived that in the course of the Revolution American society had become irretrievably diverse and selfish. Neither reality nor his theory left him any choice but to accept this fact, however horrible its implications. "The latent causes of faction are thus sown in the nature of man; and we see them everywhere brought into different degrees of activity, according

to the different circumstances of civil society. A zeal
for different opinions concerning religion, concerning
government, and many other points, as well of speculation as of practice; an attachment to different leaders ambitiously contending for preeminence and power; or to persons of other descriptions whose fortunes
have been interesting to the human passions, have, in
turn, divided mankind into parties, inflamed them
with mutual animosity, and rendered them much
more disposed to vex and oppress each other, than to
cooperate for their common good. So strong is this
propensity of mankind, to fall into mutual animosi-
ties, that where no substantial occasion presents itself, the most frivolous and fanciful distinctions have
been sufficient to kindle their unfriendly passions and
excite their most violent conflicts."

Property was of course the interest which caused
the most conflicts. But Madison accepted this interest
and the resultant clashes over property as inevitable
results of the sanctity of the individual. Take property from the individual, thought Madison, and he
cannot remain secure.

Madison was more concerned about the danger
that a majority of sacred but selfish individuals might
gain control of the government and so tyrannize a
minority. The tyrannous majority was sensed to be as
much a danger in a scheme which worshiped the striving individual as it had been in earlier visions of popular sovereignty which had worshiped the people in

their localities as sanctified by God. In either case a majority of men must rule and they might rule badly. This, to Madison, was more a problem than the continuing realities of social diversity and of open clashes over property. Selfish men might acquire governmental power and use it to abuse others. That was patently wrong.

The solution was to create a government where power was so dispersed between state and federal authorities, and among the Senate, the House of Representatives, the president, and the judiciary on the federal level, that even though nearly every body of government was elected, these were elected at such different times and from such different and often large and diverse districts that no single selfish interest could penetrate all the districts and at one and the same time elect all the bodies of this dispersed government. Checks and balances between governmental institutions, in election times and within electoral districts, meant that although a transient interest might gain control of parts of the governments of several states, and even elect a majority of the House of Representatives and possibly a president, nonetheless the governments of the other states, the federal Senate, only one-third of whose members were chosen at each election, and the federal judiciary would still have the power to restrain that potentially dangerous transient majority. It was a government designed to protect an individualistic and a democratic society from its own worst excesses.

Madison put it more dramatically: "The influence of factious leaders may kindle a flame within their particular states, but will be unable to spread a general conflagration through the other states: a religious sect may degenerate into a political faction in a part of the confederacy; but the variety of sects dispersed over the entire face of it, must secure the national councils against any danger from that source: a rage for paper money, for an abolition of debts, for an equal division of property, or for any other improper or wicked project, will be less apt to pervade the whole body of the union than a particular member of it; in the same proportion as such a malady is more likely to taint a particular county or district, than an entire state."

It was a puzzling and chilly world which Madison depicted. The comforts of wise leaders – ordained as much by God as by the people, and discerning of the public good – were gone. So were the snug securities of a sanctified localism united on all fronts against the presumptions of higher authorities. There was no God in Madison's world, only the individual. Assembled as a majority, even individuals could be dangerous. So Madison had helped assemble and was now promoting a complex democratic government secure even against such a majority. Outside this government individuals sought to realize themselves, among other things by acquiring property, amidst self-created storms of self-interest, in a society irretrievably selfish and diverse. It was a terrible vision, from which Madison later retreated into platitudes about wise leadership.

Yet Madison's was an alternative to a hierarchialism outmoded in the tides of revolution, and to a localism reborn as popular sovereignty and utterly unaware of the rights of individuals. Caught between the presumptions of "aristocracy" and the anarchy of localism, neither of which was able to achieve true legitimacy, Madison had sought a way out which would protect the individual, preserve democracy, and provide by its very complexity some source of a structured elected leadership. By and large he succeeded. In subsequent years his vision of an individualistic and diverse society, democratically electing a checked and balanced yet powerful government, has become that principle of political authority which has been accepted by most Americans most of the time.

There is considerable evidence that Americans were prepared by the Revolution to fit that framework which Madison sketched. The debates of the Revolution, the clashes of political principle and of self-interest which exploded from these, and the very language of human rights and individual choice which came to the lips of all parties may have jarred

other Americans than Madison away from the old
clichés of hierarchy or of localism into that striving
world of individuals which Madison described. In the
course of the nineteenth century, migration and im-
migration would confirm that world.

ॐ

In its persistences and in its changes the seventeenth-
and eighteenth-century American past was a more
universal world than this story has told. In New England, for example, there endured throughout this
period many universal features of life on the land in
the preindustrial past. In Salem, or in Springfield, or
in Dorchester, on a March morning, a farmer left his
small, dark house and trudged through muddy wagon
tracks to a village meeting. There his elected selectmen proposed ways to improve the roads, to care for
the poor, and to meet the military levies of the colony
in time of war. He and his neighbors discussed these,
approved them, perhaps heard a sermon, and went
home to ready the harness, plow, and servant boy for
spring plowing. Five thousand miles away in Bjursås,
or Vänäs, or Torsång, on a March morning, a farmer
(bonde) left his small, dark house (hus, bondgård)
and trudged through muddy wagon tracks to a village
meeting (bylag). There his elected selectmen (nämde-
män) proposed ways to improve the roads, to care for
the poor, and to meet the military levies of the province in time of war. He and his neighbors discussed
these, approved them, perhaps heard a sermon, and

went home to ready the harness, plow, and servant boy (dräng) for spring plowing. In Sweden there was a little more snow. Some of these same features must have been found in Virginia. The evolution of this world was slow and its features often universal. In some respects it has never left us, only changed its motives a little to meet new contexts. As the Madisonian future described here emerged, it, too, was universal. Madison was only one of several Americans to perceive a new world coming and to describe the more fluid social order in which neither communalism nor aristocratic hierarchies were appropriate. Even though they were not motivated by as paralytic a clash of localism and hierarchy as occurred in America, European intellectuals had already begun groping toward this same vision. Americans would emerge in their own convulsive way from a universal past into a universal future.

∾

Out of the debris of vulnerable legitimacies Madison had helped create what would become a universal legitimacy. Today, Americans stand in turn amidst the debris of Madison's legitimacy. The unlimited individual acquisition of property vexed them until they could not endure its inequalities any longer. Something of Madison's sacred individual had to disappear so that all could get enough property to live decently. The problem is that that same maternal state which takes and gives property in the name of mutual good takes so many of the realms of choice and of chance that make life worth living. As for the tyranny of the majority, the state itself has learned to manipulate transient majorities to confirm its own actions. Ironically, as Americans stand amidst these improvements and perversions of Madison's vision, the ancient legitimacies of the colonial past are still present. The desire to be left alone in communal sanctity has never been abandoned by Americans any more than by any other people. Hierarchies will always be built of men who aspire to office, and who consider themselves anointed once they succeed. Persons of these several inclinations never quite accepted Madison's world. Today these conflicting desires arise in new forms in reaction to a world which sometimes seems even more complicated than Madison's.

# *An essay on the sources*

SCHOLARS in early American history will rec- ognize most of the documents and secondary sources on which this interpretation is based. Lay readers, however, might be interested in some of the more recent published collections of documents and in the major interpretive works by historians which have influenced the essay.

John Demos's *Remarkable Providences, 1600–1760* (New York, 1972) has been a great influence. The documents of ordinary life included here are so full of fascinating implications that the brief introductions allowed the editor only to begin to do them justice. The reader will recognize in these letters, diaries, memoirs, and state and legal papers on early American life many of the characters in this book. John Demos deserves great credit for all the insights his collection offers.

Several other recent collections have provided important background for this book. Jack P. Greene's *Great Britain and the American Colonies, 1606–1763* (New York, 1970) begins with a brilliant essay on the evolution of the British Empire prior to the American Revolution and follows this up with a varied and sensitive collection of documentary evidence. Two collections of sources on the Great Awakening, *The Great Awakening: Documents Illustrating the Crisis and Its Consequences*, edited by Alan Heimert and Perry Miller (New York, 1967), and *The Great Awakening: Documents on the Revival of Religion, 1740–1745*, edited by Richard S. Bushman (New York, 1970), have been very useful, although this author takes a different interpretive line.

The chapter on New England owes a special debt to Perry Miller and Thomas Johnson, eds., *The Puritans: A Source Book of their Writings* (2 volumes, New York, 1963). Of outstanding use, among the thousands of more specialized volumes of published documents on New England which have been accumulating over nearly two centuries, is Edmund S. Morgan's edition of *The Diary of Michael Wigglesworth, 1653–1657* (New York, 1965). Like too many of the modern editions cited here, this volume has just gone out of print. In all cases, this is a loss to the student, as these vivid materials give ready access to a time otherwise difficult of access. Another useful collection, *The Glorious Revolution in America*, edited by Michael G. Hall, Lawrence H. Leder, and Michael G. Kammen (New York, 1964), throws light on the political crisis preceding the witchcraft trials in Massachusetts. Replies from the Massachusetts towns on the proposed state constitutions of 1778–80 can be found in Robert Taylor, ed., *Massachusetts: Colony to Commonwealth* (Chapel Hill, 1961).

Numerous secondary works have been helpful in framing an overall view of the history of New England. Timothy Breen's "Persistent Localism: English Social Change and the Shaping of New England Institutions," *William and Mary Quarterly* (January, 1975), gave a whole new dimension to a localism which many scholars had remarked upon and few had fully understood until Breen's article appeared. This localism gained still other dimensions in Paul Boyer and Stephen Nissenbaum's superb book on the witchcraft episode, *Salem Possessed* (Cambridge, Massachusetts, 1974). Their book in turn has links to an article by K. Lockridge, "Social Change and the Meaning of the American Revolution," *Journal of Social History* (Summer, 1973). (The cynical interpretation of the Mathers' role in the witchcraft trials is based on a nearly explicit statement to this effect, with evidence in support of it, offered by David D. Hall in *The Faithful Shepherd: A History of the New England Ministry in the Seventeenth Century* (Chapel Hill, 1972), pp. 245–6.) Further dimensions of localism just before the Revolution can be glimpsed in Richard S. Bushman's *From Puritan to Yankee: Character and the Social Order in Connecticut, 1690–1765* (Cambridge, Massachusetts, 1967), and these are expanded at length in Gregory Nobles's Ph.D. dissertation, "Politics and Society in Hampshire County, Massachusetts, 1740–1775" (University of Michigan, 1979, available from University Microfilms). In New England as elsewhere in the colonies, the final confirmation that localism was a vital force comes from Gordon S. Wood's matchless book on the American Revolution, *The Creation of the American Republic* (Chapel Hill, 1969). This essay on localism and hierarchy has gained immensely from the retrospective light thrown on early American history by *The Creation of the American Republic*.

Documentary sources on earliest Virginia have appeared most recently in *The Old Dominion in the Seventeenth Century: A Documentary History of Virginia, 1606–1689*, edited by Warren M. Billings (Chapel Hill, 1975). This is a far more flexible, versatile, and subtle collection than its initial institutional focus indicates. Robert Beverley's *The History and Present State of Virginia* is available in a modern edition edited by David Freeman Hawke (New York, 1971), but the most modern edition of William Byrd's *History of the Dividing Line*, edited by Louis B. Wright Gloucester, Massachusetts, 1973), seems to be out of print, as is the section of Byrd's diary used here, *The Great American Gentleman: The Secret Diary of William Byrd of Westover, 1709–1712*, edited by Louis B. Wright and Marion Tinling (New York, 1963). These and older editions can, of course, be found in libraries. Devereux Jarratt is best found in an excerpt edited by Douglass Adair, "The Autobiography of the Reverend Devereux Jarratt, 1732–1763," in the *William and Mary Quarterly* (July, 1952).

Many new articles and books have reshaped our understanding of the colonial South. Russell Menard's work, as in "From Servant to Freeholder: Status Mobility and Property Accumulation in Seventeenth-Century Maryland," *William and Mary Quarterly* (January, 1973), has led this reinterpretation of early Southern history. The trend culminated recently in *American Slavery, American Freedom: The Ordeal of Colonial Virginia* (New York, 1975), by Edmund S. Morgan, a book which sets the stage for the evolution of order out of chaos in early Virginia. The later fate of the gentry order which evolved is best seen in Rhys Isaac's seminal article, "Evangelical Revolt: The Nature of the Baptist's Challenge to the Traditional Order in Virginia, 1765 to 1775," *William and Mary Quarterly* (July, 1974). From Timothy Breen's article on New England localism to Rhys Isaac's piece on the Baptists, the interpretation offered here makes a single arch. The capstone, as in the study of New England, is Gordon Wood's *The Creation of the American Republic*.

Certain secondary works, such as Gary Nash, *Quakers and Politics: Pennsylvania, 1681–1726* (Princeton, 1968) and, for New York, Patricia U. Bonomi, *A Factious People: Politics and Society in Colonial New York* (New York, 1971), hint at the localism-of-interests which threatened hierarchy in the middle colonies. But here, too, as America entered the Revolution, the crucial reference is *The Creation of the American Republic*. Any doubt as to the overall interpretation offered here is resolved by Wood's account of an epic struggle between an archaic and corrosive localism and outmoded and astonished aristocrats for control of the American Revolution. The pervasiveness of this contest can be seen further in Jackson Turner Main, *Political Parties Before the Constitution* (Chapel Hill, 1973).

# Index

# INDEX

legitimacy (*cont.*)
  England, 109–10
  hierarchy, 50, 51–2, 103–4
  indentured servitude, 65
  law, 107
  Madison, 120–1
  "natural" men, 67
  New England/South compared,
    102
  planters, 74–6
  quest for, 3–4
  South, 69–71
  state, 92–3
  Virginia, 58, 71–4
  vulnerability of, 94, 104, 105
Levellers, 51
liberty
  aristocracy, 90
  localism, 51
  outlivers, 42–3
  slavery, 86
  Winthrop on, 21–2
localism
  American Revolution, 111–12
  community/hierarchy dichotomy,
    39
  corruption, 36
  Europe, 119–20
  evangelicalism, 42–6, 103, 106, 107
  hierarchy, 111
  individualism, 51
  legitimacy, 3, 4
  Madison, 117, 119
  milieu of, 50–1, 105–6
  New England, 8
  New England/South compared,
    102–3
  pluralism, 107–8
  politicization of, 103
  Puritanism, 36–8
  varieties of, 49–50
  *see also* backcountry
London, 8

"lubberland," *see* backcountry
Luther, Martin, 9

Machiavelli, 9
Madison, James, 112, 120–1, 113–19
majority rule, *see* minority rights
marriage and family, 22, 67, 82, 86
Maryland, 60, 61, 62–3, 65, 68, 83,
  90
Massachusetts, 47, 48–9
Mather, Cotton, 28, 31, 32, 34, 35,
  103, 110
Mather, Increase, 31, 32, 103, 110
Matthiessen, F. O., 55n
merchants, *see* commercialism
Methodist revival, 99
  *see also* Baptist revival; evangel-
    icalism
middle colonies, 107
minority rights, 114, 115–16, 121
mobility, 67
moderation, 25–6
monarchy, 41
More, Sir Thomas, 9–12, 13, 15, 16
Morgan, Edmund S., 3
Morison, Samuel Eliot, 11n
mortality rates, 82
Munster (Germany), 45

Navigation Acts, 68, 76, 82–3, 109
New England, 4, 86, 94, 106
  Byrd on, 96–7
  England and, 31–2, 38, 40–1
  ideals of, 7
  legitimacy, 3
  South compared, 68–9
Newport, Captain, 56, 58, 59, 70
New York, 107
Nissenbaum, Stephen, 3
North Carolina, 61–2, 83, 95, 96
Norwood, Harry, 77
Noyes, Nicholas, 29–30, 31, 32, 33